RUNES QUICK REFERENCE

Fehu — *Fulfillment / Rising Spiral*	Uruz — *Strength / Empowerment*	Thurisaz — *Gateway*	Ansuz — *Signals / Divine Muse*
• Ambitions satisfied • Think about what profit/gain mean to you • Wealth, possessions or self rule? • Vigilance, conserve what is gained REVERSE • Frustration • Dispossession, falling short • Ask, what do I need to learn • Shadow side of possession	• Termination and new beginning • Change in present life allows new life to be released • Rune of passage • Opportunity disguised as loss REVERSE: • Your strength may be used against you • Missed opportunity • Jolt out of un-awareness • Everything is a cycle	• Rune of non-action • Brink of contact with Universe • Review your past prior to passing through the gate • Observe all, bless all, release all • Makes stronger the ability to wait REVERSE • Quickening of development • Don't suffer over your suffering • Avoid hasty decision or act from weakness	• Gifts, timely warnings • Awareness of connections, interactions, meetings, chance encounters • Unpleasant circumstances teach • Focus on self change • Connection w/divine, Loki • Self care allows care for others REVERSE: • Concern re: failed communication • Unwillingness to take what is offered

Raido — *Communication / Soul's Journey*	Kano — *Opening / Transformational Knowledge*	Gebo — *Partnership / Energetic Exchange*	Wunjo — *Joy / Fellowship*
• Attunement of something that has two sides or elements • Ultimate union at the end of a Journey • Inner Worth • Don't rely totally on your own power REVERSE • Ruptures more likely than reconciliations • Keep your good humor • Growth requirements are disruptive	• Renewed clarity, dispelling darkness • Seriousness, clear intent • Beginnings, mutual openness in relationship • Light to see what is trivial REVERSE • Darkening of a situation/relationship • Aspect of self no longer appropriate • Relationship ending • Inner stability needed • Live empty for a time	• Don't collapse into the union • True partnership, separate/whole beings choosing to unite • Union with higher self • The divine in all things NO REVERSE	• Difficult times are over • Expected shift has occurred • Material and/or spiritual Blessing • Heightened sense of well being • New energy previously blocked REVERSE • Slowness in fruition • Crisis, difficult passage (brief) • Everything is a test • Focus in the present

Hagalaz — *Disruption, Hail / Strong Will*	Nauthiz — *Constraint, Self Reliance*	Isa — *Ice, Standstill / Contemplation*	Jera — *Harvest / Natural Cycles*
• Change, freedom, invention and liberations • Events that seem beyond our Control • Operates through reversal • The Great Awakener • Your inner strength is guidance • The more severe the disruption, the more significant for your life NO REVERSE	• Dealing with severe constraint • ID and work with your shadow side • Don't take this world personally • Use restraint, pay off debts REVERSE • A great teacher disguised as bringer of pain/limitation • Disowned parts can wreak havoc • Recognize creative power of self	• You may be blind to a situation • You may feel powerless • A freeze or drain on energy • Sacrifice cherished desire • Discover what you are holding onto and let go • Shed, cleanse, release to bring thaw • Seed of new is present in shell of the old NO REVERSE	• Beneficial Outcome • A span of time (units of 3) i.e. 3 minutes, 3 days • Full cycle before reaping • Cultivate/Persevere • Patience is essential NO REVERSE

RUNES QUICK REFERENCE

Eihwaz
Defense
Experience

- Power to avert blockage & defeat
- Delays may prove beneficial
- Patience, don't be over-eager
- A time of waiting
- Difficulties at the beginning of new life
- Able to foresee consequences
- Growth is happening - even if inconvenient or uncomfortable

NO REVERSE

Perth
Mystery
Initiation
Secrets

- Becoming whole. Renewal of spirit
- Powerful forces of change - beyond human power
- Surprises, gains, rewards
- Let go - No exceptions

REVERSE
- Don't expect too much
- The old has come to an end
- Call in scattered energies
- Be present

Algiz
Protection
Personal Space

- Control of emotions
- Accelerated self change, transition
- Do not collapse self into emotions
- Battle with self
- Don't deny what is happening
- Timely right action is only protection

REVERSE
- Be thoughtful of your health
- Take responsibility for actions
- Be aware of associations, especially when others use you

Sowelu
Wholeness
Immortality
Hope

- Rune of power, makes life force available
- Self realization, life paths originating from core of individuality
- Become conscious of your essence, bring it into form
- Regeneration down to cellular level
- Do without doing, stay focused without manipulation

NO REVERSE

Teiwaz
SpiritualWarrior
Divinity in
Humanity

- Battle always with the self
- Will through action (Yang)
- (Man of La Mancha)
- Unattached to outcomes
- Sun, Masculine Energy

REVERSE
- Life force leaking away
- Examine your motives
- Answers within
- Trust and confidence at issue

Berkana
Growth
Rising
Vibrations

- Fertility, at flow of being into their new form
- Gentle, penetrating, pervasive
- Disperse resistance than complete
- Modesty, patience, fairness called for

REVERSE
- Events or character trait interfere with your growth
- Examine what is happening, your part, other roles.

Ehwaz
Movement
Unbreakable
Bonds

- Physical shifts, new houses, attitudes, relationships, new life
- Gradual Development
- Moral effort and steadfastness
- You've progressed enough to feel secure

REVERSE
- There are not missed opportunities
- Not all opportunities are appropriate
- What is yours will come to you

Mannez
Self,
Source

- Self balances self
- Modesty
- Be non-judgmental
- Be Present
- Wunjo embedded in Mannez
- Nothing in excess

REVERSE: Blockage
- Be clear with yourself, look within
- Enemies are outer reflection of inner energies
- You are always beginning

Laguz
Flow, Abundant
Life Force

- Unseen powers that nourish, shape and connect
- Fluidity, water, ebb & flow of emotion, careers and relationships
- Immerse yourself without judging
- Satisfaction of emotional needs
- Intuitive / Lunar. Self aligning to self

REVERSE
- Don't exceed your own strength
- Failure to draw upon wisdom of instinct - you may be out of balance

Inguz
New Beginning
Beacon of Light

- Moon - Intuition
- New Life Path, joyful deliverance
- Emergence
- Harmonizing in personal relationships
- Completion of Beginnings
- free self from ruts & bad influences
- Completion is crucial

NO REVERSE

Daggaz
Breakthrough
Transformation

- Day, transformation, 180° turn
- Major shift on path to self change
- Radical trust
- Leap empty handed into the void
- Outcome assured, timing is right
- Major period of achievement and prosperity
- Do the work before you joyfully

NO REVERSE

Othilla
Separation
Inheritance
Energetic Fences

- Shed old skin, radical severance
- Acquisition and benefit
- Inheritance from something given up
- Becoming more truly who you are

REVERSE:
- Not bound by old conditioning
- Total honesty, adaptability, skill
- consider what will benefit others
- Wait for the universe to act

Odin
Unlimited
Potential

- The end, the beginning, Unlimited Potential
- Total Trust
- Portends death but generally only a symbolic death
- Relinquishing control
- No control over what has not yet taken form

NO REVERSE

BEFORE THERE WERE WORDS

WERE WORDS

THE ENERGETIC MEANINGS OF RUNES

BEFORE THERE WERE WORDS
The Energetic Meanings of Runes

KRISS ERICKSON

SYNCLECTIC MEDIA

Published by **Synclectic Media**
Seattle, Washington
www.synclectic.com

Publisher's Cataloging-in-Publication Data

Erickson, Kriss
  Before There Were Words: The Energetic Meanings of Runes / Kriss Erickson. – 1st ed.
    p. cm. –
  Summary: Before There Were Words: The Energetic Meanings of Runes, describes the mystical process of doing a Rune reading in a simple, straightforward way. This text offers something that other Rune books don't: a clear breakdown of the energetic meanings of these ancient, beautiful symbols, with personal examples to provide practical examples of how this symbolic wisdom is helpful in everyday life.
  Library of Congress Control Number: 2012935763
  ISBN: 978-0615619408
  [1. Runes—Miscellanea.] I. Title.
133.3'3—dc21   P-CIP

---

10 9 8 7 6 5 4 3 2 1
Ω
First Edition
Printed in the United States

This book is dedicated to my husband Michael,
who introduced me to the Runes, and who
created the Runic artwork in this volume.

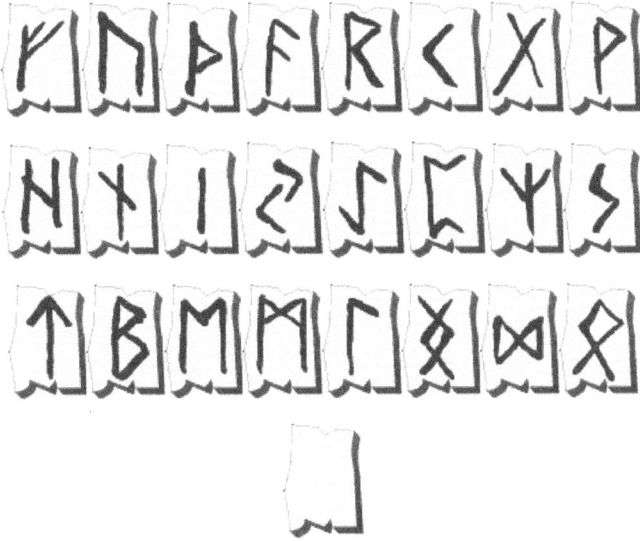

ᚠᚢᚦᚨᚱᚲᚷᚹ
ᚺᚾᛁᛃᛇᛈᛉᛊ
ᛏᛒᛖᛗᛚᛜᛞᛟ
ᛁ

10% of the publisher's proceeds from *Before There Were Words* will be donated to:

ExtraTerrestrials
http://extraterrestrials.ning.com/

Contents:

Introduction

Much of the prevailing information about one of the most ancient alphabets, the Nordic Runes, has a tendency to make the simply-carved shapes seem strange and complicated. In some ways, the Runes are mysterious, yet only as mysterious as we allow our own inner wisdom to be.

As Ted J. Kaptchuk, O.M.D. puts it, "Wisdom is a recognition of a deep knowing that infuses life."[1]

The truth is, we all have a deep knowing of the energies that make up our lives. We may call it intuition or "gut feeling" but it is there, waiting for us to call upon it. We just aren't taught to think about our inner wisdom on a conscious level. The deep wisdom of the Runes may seem mysterious until we realize that this deep wisdom speaks to our own deepest yearning—to connect our inner and outer lives and to understand what has brought us to our current place in life.

Runes as Guides

In the years that I've been reading Runes, these ancient archetypal symbols have offered me insight and wisdom about how I came to be in the place I am in now. What decisions did I make six months ago, for instance, that led me to either an enjoyable or a not-so enjoyable place?

---

[1] Kaptchuk, Ted J., O.M.D., *The Web that Has No Weaver*, p. 86.

An example of how the Runes have informed me of the patterns I've set into motion in my life came when I was beginning my graduate studies. I was so sure of my choice of schools that I didn't want to consult the Runes. Yet a niggling voice of intuition in the back of my head urged me to do so.

Finally, I complied by choosing a three-Rune cast for the situation, simply asking (Rune 1) What can I expect from this situation, (Rune 2) What is my best course of action and (Rune 3) What is the potential outcome if I ignore my intuition and attend this grad school?

I came up with Nauthiz, Rune of Constraint and Self-Reliance, Isa, Rune of Stillness and Contemplation and Hagalaz, Rune of Disruption and Strong Will.

Nauthiz warned that if I went to my chosen grad school, I would feel bound by tightly-held yet not clearly obvious beliefs and traditions of the school. This Rune also urged me to rely on myself instead of on how prestigious others felt my attendance at the school would be.

Isa urged me not to make a hasty decision. This Rune also cautioned me that if I moved too quickly and didn't take the time to consult my inner wisdom that the sense of constraint and restriction indicated in the first Rune, Nauthiz, would be accentuated, making me even more uncomfortable.

Hagalaz warned that if I didn't listen to my inner wisdom, that my life would be disrupted. If I was determined to attend this school, I would be able to successfully complete the course of study, but through cleverness on my part, not because my energy would be harmonious with that of the school.

Well, I chose to ignore the message of the Runes and of my inner wisdom. And the next three years were an exercise of endurance. I did finish my studies, earning a Master of Arts in Counseling, but this outcome came at great personal expense that was manifested in my confidence and personal beliefs being constantly challenged by the professors and my fellow students.

Deeply Simple Tools

This example shows the deeply simple nature of the Runes. Runes have the ability to indicate patterns of energy that we set into motions in our lives because of the decisions we make. This doesn't make them complicated.

The word I would use for the Runes is multifaceted because of the layered knowledge inherent in each Rune that speaks to the matters closest to our hearts and sense of being. To describe the Runes as complicated creates a barrier between the individual and the Runes that doesn't need to exist.

I'd like this book to be an opportunity for anyone interested in Rune lore to see the connection between the Runic symbols and the main archetypes and energetic themes of the universe. The more you work with and know the Runes, the more information they will offer and the more help they will bring to help you to know your inner self.

Archetypal Nature of Runes

Since the Runes are archetypes, they're more than an alphabet and yet an extremely effective way of communicating themes, thoughts, ideas and concepts through a series of twenty-four symbols plus one blank. Runes also make up a symbolic language that can form words.

For example, I used four Runes to form a word at the beginning of this chapter. A bit of Runic "graffiti" if you will. The word I created for this chapter was, "Life," made using Laguz, Isa, Fehu and Ehwaz. The modern English word that combination of Runes spells is indicated by the first letter of each of the names of the Runes.

As an energetic reading, this group of Runes would hold the themes of: the overall flow of life, the deep contemplation necessary to live a balanced life, the sense of value placed on our own lives and on life in general and how well we are able to move into the opportunities and experiences that make up our lives.

So even as graffiti, the Runes form a cohesive message that can guide and inform.

Runes as Symbols

Symbolic languages have existed since pre-historic times, when humankind first became aware of an inner need to be connected to a bigger reality. The first forms of language were an attempt to connect to symbols in the natural world that would help us to survive and create a stronger connection to the world around us and to the universe. The symbols we chose began as simple representations of natural processes that were condensed forms of information.

As such, a single ancient symbol represented an idea or life process, which allowed it to contain much more information than a single letter in our modern alphabet today. One of the reasons that I feel that Rune lore and Rune casting is such an important tool for helping us to understand ourselves and receive guidance for our lives is that when viewed archetypically, the ancient Runic alphabet is one of the richest sources of energetic thread knowledge that exists.

The Origins of Symbolic Language

How did we arrive at being able to not only recognize the importance of symbols and create representations of symbols to communicate with, but to identify the layers of wisdom and knowledge contained in each?

One source of symbolic information was the natural world. Watching the natural world taught people about structure, the cyclic nature of life and the interconnection between the elements, animals, plants and people.

The moon grew and shrank each month. Trees bloomed in the spring, leafed out in summer, created fruit and colorful cascades in autumn and stood unashamedly naked in the winter. Water gave life to plants, people and animals, and could also be a destructive force in times of flood, as well as a sought-after blessing in times of drought.

Our human ancestors soon learned that if they watched and learned from the symbols of the natural world, they could understand how the world worked and how to live in it. So our ancestors watched the ebb and flow of the seasons, the migrations of animals and birds, listened to the wind and followed the currents of the water. The languages and symbols they developed reflected this focus.

Another source in the development of a symbolic language was the need to communicate. Yes, gestures could be made. Words could be spoken. But how to remember from one season to the next which areas the deer moved through, or which meadows produced the most edible greens each spring? How to leave a record for future generations to learn from and add to?

The elements are the natural world's way of communicating with us without words. As a race, we learned from these natural processes, but we needed more. Soon, we began creating symbols to communicate. While many of those symbols had their origins in the elements of the natural world, the information they conveyed had a combined meaning of the information from the elements, the Universe and the meanings humankind added to them to speak to our own needs.

What Kinds of Symbols Were Used?

Many kinds of symbols were used, but most showed a universally known object or idea. For example, a squiggle drawn with a stick in the dust could indicate a river. A straight line could represent a tree or a path. A circle could mean a piece of fruit or the sun. Each symbol represented an object, an idea and a message that needed to be conveyed.

Symbolic languages varied in complexity and appearance. But again, the intricate nature of the human rationale behind language made even the simplest looking alphabets deceptively complex. The simplest symbols used for communication were a series of short and long slanted lines and dots, called Ogam[2].

Ogam may be one of the oldest alphabets but it is hardly the simplest. The possibilities for the patterns of lines and dots are nearly endless, making translating Ogam a monumental challenge. Still, the development of Ogam was an important step in the development of an alphabet.

The Development of Runes

Over the centuries, human language and alphabets continued to be refined. Runes, among the oldest alphabets, were created by the Norse peoples of Northern Europe for use in divination and reading a person's life energy, which was considered a form of magic[3] and as such, are deeply connected to Norse mythology.

Runes were also used as an alphabetic script, though their connection to divine messages from the gods and

---

[2] http://www.encyclopedia.com/doc/1O245-ogam.html
[3] Penneck, Nigel, *The Complete Illustrated Guide to Runes: How to Interpret the Ancient Wisdom of the Runes*, p. 25.

goddesses, beginning about two thousand years ago[4], caused squabbles around Rune usage that were more superstitious than practical in nature. As late as the seventeenth-century in Iceland, a person could be executed for owning Runes.[5]

Though Runes were initially intended to guide people on their energetic and spiritual paths, they were also a stable and dependable way to convey meaning, create words and messages.

Runes as a Symbolic Language

I hope you can see even from this brief introduction that Runes are much more than a set of symbols like our alphabet, used to create words. Each Rune is a symbol sent from the Universe to help us become more aware of and to illuminate the energetic paths of our lives.

Because of this energetic factor, Runes contain elements of the earliest, pre-alphabetic natural symbols that intuitively connected our ancestors to the natural world and elements of symbolic communication similar to, if less complex, than Ogam.

When I speak of complexity, I don't mean that the simpler-looking set of twenty-four Elder Runes and one Blank Rune that was added at a later date are less complex than Ogam or other ancient alphabets in their symbolic language. Runes are condensed, so that a person may learn many life lessons from a single Runic character.

While other alphabets, such as the Magdalenian, Phoenician and Egyptian hieroglyphic, were developed centuries before the Runes[6], Runes are significant because

---

[4] Wiccan-world.com http://www.wiccan-world.com/reference_d_f/futhark_runes/futhark_runes.html
[5] Penneck, Nigel, *The Complete Illustrated Guide to Runes*, p. 25.
[6] Pennick, Nigel, The Complete Illustrated Guide to Runes, p.8.

they were one of the precursors to the modern Western alphabet.

As such, each Rune symbol is a thematic instrument to guide people not only to a specific message but also to share insight into overall life paths. The main focus of the Runes is on the development of the inner self. Inner balance creates a life of health, happiness, fulfillment, peace and wealth.

The Thematic Nature of Runes

I believe the thematic aspect of Runes grew at least in part out of an observation of nature. A major source of Shamanic wisdom and knowledge has come from the careful observance of the natural world and natural cycles of birth, growth, maturity, fruition, death and rebirth.

Trees drop their leaves in the autumn, looking more like sticks than living plants. This brings to mind one of the simplest Runic symbols, the single straight line that represents the Rune Isa.

It would be logical to think that a single line would have a straightforward meaning. But as with all Runes, the themes of Isa are varied. For example, Isa can indicate energy that is stagnant or fearful, indicating a need for warming energy to melt it so the affected person can interact more freely with life again.

But Isa can also indicate a time for deep contemplation, renewal and rest. Moments of stillness in life are as necessary as the winter months are in the natural cycle. Though a tree may look dormant in winter, its roots are busily gathering energy for spring. Meditation and contemplation in quiet moments of our lives can provide us with a respite from hectic schedules as well as the opportunity to get into deeper contact with our inner wisdom, so that we are ready to leap forward when the energy shifts.

There is an element of trust in Isa as well. Trees give up everything they have except their bare skeletons as they prepare to rest in the winter. Far from creating weakness, the empty-limbed tree stands tall and straight, gathering strength through its roots to create new leaves in the spring.

This is a reminder to us that the quieter or emptier cycles of our lives are nothing to be afraid or ashamed of, but are part of a natural pattern. As with all Runes, Isa holds a choice. Will we stand calmly secure in the core of our identity as we are stripped bare to face the colder times in our own lives, or will we panic and try to cover ourselves with things that we no longer need?

Another example of a natural symbol is the Rune Algiz. Algiz looks like the antler of a deer. Antlers protect the deer from predators and help the bucks to create boundaries between herds. So we can that see the element of choice in Algiz is in how we will defend ourselves. We have the choice of offensive attack or of setting clear boundaries.

Algiz reminds us that while it's safe and healthy for us to create boundaries in our lives, there are also times when we must defend ourselves more rigorously. Which is our wisest choice in our current circumstance? Which energetic thread of the Rune of defense will serve us best?

Another simple Runic symbol is the Warrior Rune, Teiwaz. Teiwaz looks like an upward pointing arrow. As an arrow this symbol can point to an object or indicate which direction to take to get to the nearest town. As a symbol, Teiwaz reminds us that we each have a warrior inside of us that helps us to stand tall while reminding us that we are always able to draw upon the strength of the universe.

The choice in this Rune is which direction to point the arrow. Will we focus our energy upward, toward the unlimited Source energy of the universe, or downward, limiting ourselves to the resources that humankind can create?

And, don't forget that Teiwaz isn't a one-way street. We can point the arrow where it is needed, then, once we have learned what we can from following that direction, we may choose to point it again. A main lesson is to keep our path straight. Make a choice, then follow that direction as far as is practical.

Loki

Links to Gods and Goddesses

Runes are also one of the direct links to God and Goddess energy. The ancient tribes that lived in northern Europe, including the Germans, Goths and Anglo-Saxons, viewed the world as a challenge to the inner spirit. They saw the Gods and Goddesses as a superior Race because they had proven themselves to be able to master and even conquer the elements of earth, water, air, metal, fire and spirit.

Among the Gods and Goddesses represented by the Runes are the Trickster God Loki, associated with the Rune

Ansuz; Ing, the Hero God, associated with the Rune Inguz; Tiw, the Sky God, associated with the Rune Teiwaz; Thor, associated with the Rune Thurisaz and Odin, the All-Father, associated with the Blank or Odin Rune.

The Question of the Blank Rune

The earliest versions of the Runes, called the Elder Futhark, named after the first six Runes in the Runic alphabet, didn't include the Blank or Odin Rune. Because of this, some Runic scholars don't consider the Blank Rune to be valid. I feel there is enough evidence, if not historically, then energetically and thematically, to include the Odin Rune when using Runes as divination tools.

Following are some of the reasons I feel the Odin Rune is not only a valid addition to the original twenty-four Runes, but also a necessary thematic and energetic symbol.

Early northern European legends agree with the Christian Bible that in the beginning there was a void—a blank space[7]. This blank space, this space of unlimited potential, representing the end of a period of darkness and the beginning of a new world, is personified by the Norse God, Odin, and the blank Rune called the Odin Rune.

In a way, Odin encompasses the whole of Rune lore. Here lie the threads of beginnings and endings, the promise of new life after loss, the indication of the unlimited nature of the universe itself, as well as a reminder that as we weed out elements that are no longer serving us, we leave space for new things to grow. Here also is a reminder of the unlimited potential contained within the energy of each person and a reminder of our unbreakable connection to the universe.

An ancient legend says that the Norse God Odin hung by his feet on the Yggdrasil or World Tree, over a body of

---

[7] *Women's Devotional Bible*, New International Version, p.1.

water. It is said that he didn't eat or drink until he saw the Runes in the ripples of water and the reflection of the pool. Odin is also called the Great Rune Master in an Old Norse poem, The Poetic Edda.[8]

Though there are many reasons to include the Blank Rune in Rune sets, the most important reason is that the inclusion of Odin's Rune is an important way to inspire us to look into the Void. Since Runes lead us to consider aspects of the Self, the Blank Rune is a foundational energetic reminder that we are at once alone, yet one with All That Is. Over and over throughout our lives we are challenged to leap empty-handed into the Void, yet that Void is where our strength and potential lies.

Many oracles were received in this way, as representations of the powers that govern the universe. Noticing the signs of nature and delving into our own inner wisdom helps us to become aware of the energetic patterns of our own lives. Studying Runes helps us to find ways to hone the energies that we create in our lives to focus our intent and bring inner patterns to the surface just as the falling of autumn leaves is the outward manifestation of the end of the summer growth cycle.

Another reason that I skirt debates about which Runes should and shouldn't be included in Rune sets is that the Rune symbols didn't originate from human wisdom. They were born of the wisdom of the Universe, channeled through the inner wisdom of shamans and others who devoted their lives to the study of what we call insight.

According to energy healer Donna Eden, Einstein said that all matter is made up of energy.[9] Energy is constantly in motion. Even energy that is stagnant is vibrating against its confines, causing discomfort. This discomfort is not meant

---

[8] *The Book of Runes*, Ralph H. Blum, page 31-32.
[9] *Energy Medicine*, Donna Eden, page 33.

to hurt us but to raise our awareness of what needs to be done so that the trapped energy might be set free.

This would indicate that change is not only possible, but inevitable. So the fact that the Odin Rune wasn't included in the earliest branches of Rune lore doesn't mean that our use of it now is improper. Instead, it is a sign of growth and a deepening of our human understanding. To refuse to use it because we as a race weren't able to grasp its importance in our earliest attempts would be to penalize and limit our intuitive growth.

Becoming Aware of Our Energy

One of the most useful aspects of studying Runes is the deepened connection we are able to attain from focusing on archetypes and energetic messages. Everything in the universe, from the smallest molecules to the most complex beings, has an optimal rate of vibration to keep it healthy. We reach our highest vibrational level when we are whole, healthy, and fulfilling our highest potential. We're able to consciously control these vibrations within ourselves using a variety of techniques.

One technique that is helpful to maintain a high vibrational level is the use of divination tools, such as Runes, Tarot, Reiki and crystals, to increase our ability to form a clear intent and to sharpen our intuitive skills.

All things created by people begin with a clear, simple intent, or focused idea. The first time our ancient ancestors connected the action of a stone rolling downhill and realized that placing round objects under a flat piece of bark would allow them to move heavy objects more easily, the idea of a wheel was born.

Runes are a tool to hone our inner strengths, to create energetic paths to move through our lives.

Runes Developed Over Time

The introductory information I've provided here has shown how Runes developed over time. In addition to Ogam, rock carvings called "prerunic symbols"[10] have been found in northern Italy, Scandinavia, Iceland and northern Europe. As symbols, Runes are linked to the cycles of the natural year and to major life themes. Runes are intuitive tools that are concerned with the most challenging study an individual can undertake—the art of self-change.

The traditional German or elder Futhark had twenty-four Runes, which include all the Runes I'll discuss in this book, with the exception of the Blank or Odin Rune. Runes spread through trading, wars and Anglo-Saxon missionaries. As Runes became more and more widely used, standardization occurred.

The runic alphabet was called Futhark after its first six letters, as illustrated below:

"F" stands for Fehu, the Rune of abundance and wealth, or Rune of the Rising Spiral.

"U" stand for Uruz, the Rune of strength, or Rune of Empowerment.

"TH" stands for Thurisaz, the Rune of the Energetic Gateway.

"A" stands for Ansuz, Rune of Signals or Rune of the Divine Muse.

"R" stand for Raido, Rune of Journey, or Rune of the Soul's Journey.

"K" stands for Kano, the Rune of Opening and Light, or Rune of Transforming Knowledge.

As I've discussed earlier, the Blank or Odin Rune was added later. The Blank Rune stands for the overall theme of

---

[10] *The Complete Illustrated Guide to Runes*, Nigel Pennick, p.8.

the Runic alphabet—the unlimited potential the reminds us of the presence of the Divine in all things.

As intuitive tools, Runes are also healing tools—vessels of intention that call the seeker to look deeply into his or her heart to the root causes of life concerns, challenges and transitions.

In the introduction to Ralph H. Blum's The Book of Runes,[11] Dr. Martin D. Rayner urges the student of Rune lore to "learn their language and let them speak to you."

This shows the importance of intent in self-work, regardless of the tools chosen.

Consulting the Runes

When I consult the Runes, I approach them with respect, since I see them as a link to the unlimited Universal pool of wisdom and knowledge and as such, an ancient, trusted friend. The Runes don't tell us what to do or give static 'yes' or 'no' answers such as what choices we should make.

Instead of predicting the future, Runic philosophy reminds us that the future is constantly being shaped by the present and as such, can be changed moment to moment, depending on the energy we choose to direct our lives.

The most exciting aspect of the Runes is their use as energetic tools to help us sense the underlying patterns of our lives that resonate to the frequency of the themes we set in motion through our everyday choices.

Shifting our energy shifts our lives. Whenever we feel stuck, delving into the wisdom of the Runes can help us to recognize new possibilities and pathways that we may have overlooked. Runes plumb the deepest reaches of our spirit self—the Higher Self—and also urge us to look deep

---

[11] *The Book of Runes*, Ralph H. Blum, p. 8.

enough into ourselves to recognize hidden fears, motivations, and patterns.

May the Runes lead you to the breakthroughs you need to enhance your life.

Namaste.

Chapter 1:
The Energetic/Intuitive Nature of Runes

Rune casts show the elements that are contained in the energy moving through our lives or being attracted into our lives by the patterns we've created that affect each moment. Becoming more aware of the patterns we've established and/or have accepted into our lives by consulting the Runes gives us perspective by indicating possible outcomes given the present energy patterns.

Like the Runic graffiti above, the energy patterns aren't always direct. The word I spelled above would be translated as "strong." The fact that the messages contained in the word "strong" give insight into the themes of strength speaks to the thematic and individualistic nature of the Runes.

If I wanted to give the energy of strength using Runes, I wouldn't have to write it out letter by letter as we do in modern English. All I would need to do is use a single Rune, Uruz:

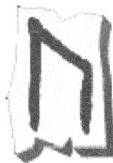

This Rune would indicate the many ideas and energetic connections around the concept of strength.

In much the same way, a Rune cast is a pattern indicator and an intuitive connection to the universe, acting like a mirror, reflecting back at us what the path is that we are traveling and where on that path we are in the present moment. The evidence of the path and the reflection are contained in the thematic messages that lie within each Rune.

Though it is possible to create words and write sentences using Runes, each Rune is more than a symbol, or a single letter. Each Rune holds a theme: selfhood, partnership, transformation, stillness, possessions, or disruption.

If I wanted to use the five Runes that literally spell "strong" in English, I would be incorporating the themes of Wholeness (Sowelu), Inner Warrior (Teiwaz), Communication (Raido), Boundaries (Othila) and having the sense of presence to allow my inner light to shine out to the world (Inguz—which represents "ng" in writing).

I could choose this route, as I did with the Runic graffiti, which would give me a lot of thematic information that would inform me about how to create a strong inner and outer life. Or I could choose to meditate on all the nuances of the archetypal information contained in the single Rune of Strength, Uruz.

I hope you can see by this example that the themes expressed through the Runes are broad enough to encompass many situations and yet are intricate enough to clarify life issues.

In a way, Runes resemble the I Ching, since they show a moving, emerging pattern as well as an indication of the origin of the present pattern and areas of potential challenge or dynamic energy. Also like the I Ching, Runes are a way to gain insight and knowledge from the wisdom of the

Universe. As Wu Wei states in the introduction to I Ching, "For us to be able to draw from the fount of Universal wisdom, we must have the means to do so."[12]

Runes are a deeply intuitive means, or way, to draw from the fount of Universal wisdom. As you work with Runes, remember that though Runes are tools to help you develop your own insight and deepen your connection to the universe, it isn't the Runes that bring the reward or insight. Runes merely remind you of the Universal themes that guide all of our lives, as well as our own inner wisdom.

While universal wisdom is always available, reward and insight, as well as disappointment and frustration, are brought by your own choices and the energies you attract into or turn away from your daily life. Studying the energetic patterns of daily life can shed light on your overall life themes and patterns, giving you the perspective of what you can expect given your present pattern and what can be done to shift direction if need be to achieve your goals.

Runes as Overall Life Energy Indicators: Heart Runes

This is where the idea of Heart Runes comes in. As a thematic tool, choosing a Rune with the intent to reveal a major energetic theme or life path can show you the subconscious decisions and choices we've made that have shaped your life.

This is possible because Runes mirror unconscious processes and motivations, giving us insight into how you came to be where you are now and where your present position may lead.

The ultimate goal of seeking out a Heart Rune is to create a deeper understanding into your life so that you will eventually be able to see the overall theme of your life. Being able to see the themes in your life is like having a road

---

12 Wu Wei, *I Ching*, page 4.

map. Seeing the overall theme of your life is like solving the major mystery of your reason for being here in this time, space and manifestation.

I've devoted a chapter to Heart Rune interpretations later on in this book, but an example of a Heart Rune could be a person who constantly creates drama in her life pulling the Rune Nauthiz as a Heart Rune. Interestingly enough, Nauthiz stands for both the pain that is created when we don't have the confidence to believe in ourselves while urging us to develop the self-reliance that will bring deep satisfaction.

Chapter 2:
Casting Runes

There are many ways to cast Runes. Some people draw a circle and scatter the Runes, reading the Runes with symbols facing upright. This is done to help ensure that the cast is as spontaneous as possible, without even subconscious ego interfering with the Runes chosen.

Some people simply reach into the Rune bag and choose the Runes for the cast. Others intuitively speak to the bag or Runes, sending a silent message for the highest good of the person seeking their wisdom, then draw the Runes.

The Runic graffiti I've chosen for this chapter is simply the word, Rune. As spelled in English, this message contains the elements of inner and outer Communication (Raido), Strength and Empowerment (Uruz), the development of Self-Reliance (Nauthiz) and the ability to Move freely through life (Ehwaz).

These elements convey the overall message of the Runes themselves: that of having the insight, support and tools to live a self-empowered life.

When I cast Runes, I invite the intuitive nature of the Runes to inform me of the patterns I have or am in the process of creating in my life. I approach the Runes with respect, as if I'm communicating with an intelligent being. Which in a way, I am, since I'm opening a channel of trust between myself and the archetypal energies contained in the Runes.

If I'm casting Runes for someone else, I first create an atmosphere of respect, opening a channel of trust the same way I do when casting Runes for myself. I then ask the seeker for an intention or concern then hold the Rune bag between my palms. I send a clear intention to the Runes, asking for Universal guidance on behalf of the seeker. My only concern is of simply on being an open channel for the Runes to speak through. This allows universal wisdom to flow for the maximum benefit of the seeker.

Once the intention is sent and the channel is open, I massage the Rune bag then let it rest on my palm until a Rune heats up. I draw Runes one by one as they heat up in the bag. I learned to do this by working with the Runes and by seeing the messages they contain as direct links to Universal wisdom. As such, I'm not literally asking a bag of stones to speak to me. I'm using the stones to indicate the threads of Universal knowledge and wisdom that are needed in each situation.

This is a practical use of intuition as well as a way to show respect for the energetic nature of the Runes. Sometimes a Rune will pop from the bottom of the bag into my hand or, as incredible as it may sound, even roll or jump out of the bag, toward the seeker.

Addressing the Runes with respect and openness combines the energies of the seeker's intention, my sincere desire to convey the universal messages, the Runic energy and the wisdom of the universe to bring a healing message. The energy connected to the Runes is the energy of life, the Wu Wei spoken of in ancient Chinese philosophy, or as Michael Mayer puts it in Energy Psychology, "effortless effort."[13]

---

[13] Michael Mayer, *Energy Psychology*, page 233.

Linking Wu Wei to the Runes echoes the ancient wisdom, "Do without doing and it gets done."[14]

In other words, the most important aspect of drawing the Runes is to be open to the energetic connection between yourself, the seeker, the Runes and the Universe.

This is the heart, not only of divination, but of healing as well, because it is the awareness that you're willing to observe the things that happen in your life in a thematic way that separates out the ego that allows you to make a deep connection to the energetic threads of the Universe. It's the energetic threads that communicate the information to your body/mind/spirit to inform you how to live in balance and harmony.

This willingness to observe awakens and strengthens the Observer Self, putting you in a place of balance where emotions are felt but not allowed to be in charge of your actions. Holding an awareness of the Observer Self also helps to keep you in a constant state of meditation that provides the perspective to act and interact from a position of wisdom and calmness instead of the drama of emotional reactions.

---

14 *The Book of Runes*, Ralph H. Blum, p. 99.

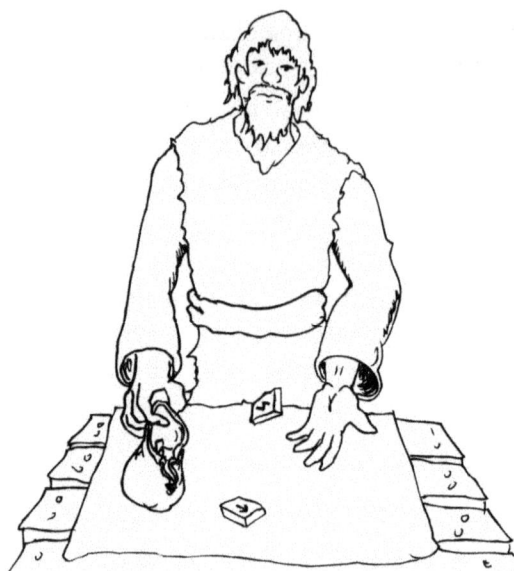

Chapter 3:
What Runes Are

Runes are tools that can be used to develop intuition.

Runes are energetic symbols.

Runes are an intuitive link to our inner selves.

Runes are a link to universal wisdom.

Runes are healing tools.

Runes are insight-linked symbols.

Runes are reflectors of the seeker's energy.

Runes open a channel that links the seeker's, the reader's and Universal energies.

Runes are wise friends and intuitive guides.

Runes urge us to become aware of our own energy and subconscious motives.

Runes are a link to our Higher Selves.
Runes are patterns within patterns.

Chapter 4:
What Runes Are Not

Runes are not tools used to prophesy.

Runes are not judgmental. There are no 'negative' or 'positive' spreads, no 'good' or 'bad' Runes, only indications of flows of energy that lead to possible outcomes.

Runes are not oracles that tell you what to do. If you're on a path of pain, it is helpful to see how and where that path began and where it is leading as well as to realize that it's a path of your own choosing.

Runes don't predict disaster, bring pain or cause any outcome.

Runes are not a way to absolve us of personal responsibilities. Rather, they challenge us to look more deeply into the patterns we have set in motion and consider the choices we've made as well as choices that could be presented to us given our current pattern.

Runes are not a way for a reader to show off intuitive skills. The more a reader relies on the wisdom of the Runes and on the information channeled from the Universe, the more helpful the message will be for the seeker.

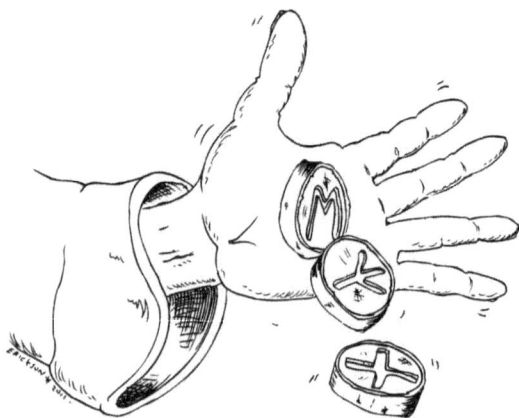

Chapter 5:
Runes and Life Cycles

Runes are tied to cycles: life cycles such as birth, manhood, womanhood, death, stillness and growth; and energetic cycles such as the need for boundaries, protection, constraint and joy.

Each of the Runes challenges us to consider the deepest levels of self-change and discover the deepest levels of truth inherent in our body/mind/spirit. Ralph H. Blum and others have identified thirteen Runes that illuminate the patterns within the pattern, so to speak—the life cycle an individual is presently in. Blum and others call these Runes Cycle Runes. I feel that all Runes can indicate life cycles and so will not limit this discussion of Runes to the thirteen Cycle Runes. Instead, I'll point out how all Runes contain information that helps those seeking wisdom from the Runes to become more aware of the cycles and patterns of their lives.

One reason I give myself a weekly Rune reading is to be aware of the cycles that are occurring in my life. I may be aware, for example, of what I need to do to prepare for the things I've chosen in my life, but what often catches me off-guard is how I'll respond to varying levels of stress.

Often when I'm preparing for a busy time, the Runes Isa and Nauthiz will show up. This used to frustrate me. How could I be still (Isa) when there was so much to do? And how could I have created a cycle where I would be constrained or restricted (Nauthiz) when I had planned so carefully?

The energy represented in these two Runes speaks to a major challenge for my life—that of developing and refining my sense of timing, specifically how patient I'm able to be with myself and others. Isa reminds me to take a few moments before I jump into my daily routine and Nauthiz reminds me that if I move too quickly I could end up skipping steps or missing details that could cost me time and effort later.

So giving yourself (or asking a friend to give you) a weekly Rune reading is one way of being aware of the cycle or cycles that are at work in your life.

Another way is to look at the life cycles represented in the Rune Cast. A good Rune Cast to use to examine life cycles is the Runic Cross. The Runic Cross has six or seven Runes:

Past

Present

Future

Underlying energy (indicating what's motivating all the actions around the present events)

Possible challenge

Possible outcome

A seventh Rune can be placed to the side of the Runic Cross as a "confirmation" Rune. What the seventh or confirmation Rune does is give a bit more insight—kind of like an extended weather forecast.

The shape of this Cast is like a cross, with the past, present and future Runes running vertically, right to left, the underlying energy Rune (Rune 4) beneath the "present" Rune (Rune 2), and the challenge and outcome Runes above the "present" Rune.

To begin to work with the energy of life cycles in a Rune cast, first look for the overall or most obvious cycle in the Rune Cast.

For example, in a Rune cast where the Runes Berkana, Kano and Fehu appear, a main cycle of that cast would be that of growth. In a Rune cast where Hagalaz, Nauthiz and Eihwaz appear, a main cycle would be that of disruption, the necessity for change and the need to strengthen boundaries.

Once you are confident that you can recognize and interpret the overall life cycle that comes up in the Rune Cast, you can begin to see and speak on how a bigger life cycle is interacting with smaller cycles and/or patterns representing the seeker's present life energy.

Including a discussion of major life energies when interpreting a Rune cast is similar to the way that the Major Arcana cards of the Tarot indicate major life patterns.

For example, say someone asks you to read the Runes to determine what would happen if they were to move to a new house. The Rune cast would pick up the overall pattern of energy in motion in the person's life, taking into account all the factors that would be affected by moving to a new house.

Their feelings about moving, including any apprehension or uncertainty as well as any excitement or joy would show in the Runes cast. If they are also in a cycle of new life, or new marriage, if children have recently been born or grown up and left home, all of these elements will be present in their overall energy signature and would be represented in the Rune cast as well.

Instead of labeling certain Runes as Cycle Runes, I feel it's more helpful and less restrictive to consider the cycles presented in the pattern of the Runes themselves. For example, if the seeker has experienced a lot of change or if the idea of change has been a recurring theme in their life, the Initiation Rune, Perth, could indicate the need for deeper exploration or that the person is in an overall state of being initiated into new phases of life.

The Rune of Separation, Othila, could indicate a new beginning, and/or an ending, both of which are present in a physical move. The pattern within the pattern also reminds the seeker that a physical move will bring emotional and energetic challenges. Pointing out overall life cycles can also help the seeker to see the bigger picture and gain perspective.

It's important also to consider when interpreting the Runes, patterns that indicate what part of a cycle the person is in. If the Message Rune, Ansuz, is drawn, for example, this could indicate the beginning of a new cycle as well as the importance of listening for messages from the Universe.

As you can see, reading the Runes isn't simply matter of looking at the messages contained in each Rune. When reading Runes, the challenge is to recognize cycles within cycles. Also be aware of the relationship between the Runes. Pay attention to Runes with similar themes. For example, if a seeker asks about a business venture, look for thematic connections in the Rune cast that address this concern.

When reading the Runes for life cycles, look for Runes that indicate stages in the seeker's life. If the Runes that are cast indicate that self-growth is emphasized, the seeker may feel an urgent desire to meet challenges or make changes in his or her life. Indeed, that may have been the catalyst that has drawn them to you in the first place.

Chapter 6:
Runes and Universal Laws

Runes were developed by shamans and other observant people who spent time contemplating universal symbols like the five elements of air, water, earth, fire and spirit and gleaning wisdom from the natural world.

Being aware of the energy and wisdom behind the elements helped mankind to learn to live well and safely. But there are deeper Laws and lessons tied to each Rune symbol. I believe that if we look at the energy behind each of the Runes, we will see that they are tied to messages of universal wisdom.

For example, many sources say that the goal and focus of Rune lore is the development and growth of the self—both the daily self and the higher self. Many of the Runes speak to the balance between the earthly self and the heavenly self, and speak of the harmony that is created when the outward and higher expressions of self come into agreement with each other.

Because of this, I have assigned a Universal Law to each Rune, in the chapter that discusses each Rune at length. You may also discover different Universal Laws to apply to the Runes that come up for you. This is a natural part of getting to know the Runic messages on an energetic level.

The Runic graffiti I've used for this chapter spells the word "Laws." Laguz (the "L") indicates the need to find your own sense of flow or rhythm in life, Ansuz (the "A") reminds us of the need to consult with others to gain wisdom and knowledge, Wunjo (the "W") shows that balanced and fair laws bring happiness and Sowelu (the "S") reminds us that we as individuals and as a society are made whole by a balance of inner and outer laws.

Being aware of the Universal Laws attached to the Runes was one of the reasons my husband, Michael, began using Runes. He noticed that when Teiwaz, Rune of the Spiritual Warrior and of the Divinity in Humanity, showed up, that the energy of this Rune reminded him to face the challenges that arose in his life. There was no judgment in the energy of this Rune that condemned him for times he didn't know how to stand up for himself, only a constant reminder that the Universe had given him inner strength to use on his own behalf.

The nonjudgmental nature of Runes can provide confidence, no matter which Runes appear, to give guidance in our lives.

Crown Chakra

Chapter 7:
Runes and Chakras

Chakra is a Sanskrit term used to describe the energetic gates connected to the vital Lifeforce in a physical body. This vital Lifeforce exists in all life forms. It animates our bodies, our minds, lets us feel emotions and make free choices. The Chakras are transformers of subtle energy. On an energetic level, the endocrine glands correspond to the seven main chakras, or energy centers.

Chakras are tied to the twelve major meridians of the body. The meridians are the way our cells, organs, and body/mind/spirit receives information.

The seven main Chakras look a little like flowers, with the petals spread on the outside of the body and the stem forming a cone that funnels energy into the body. They are aligned with the head and spinal column and act as the energetic counterpart to major organs and glands within the body. There are many minor Chakras, most of which are associated with the body's joints. Each Chakra funnels Life-force energy or Ki into the body. Each Chakra also reflects and aspect of personal growth.

How do Runes tie into the Chakra energy system?

Since the core of Runic energy comes from the energetic threads that govern the universe and since the main concern of Runes is to help us grow a stronger, calmer, more balanced and connected sense of self, the Runes drawn in a Rune cast can be used to indicate focus, balance and/or clearing needed in one or more Chakras.

How to do this is to look at the color represented by each Rune in the cast as you are sharing your interpretation.

I've found this Rune cast to be particularly powerful in helping people be aware of and make changes in the way they express their personal energy. For example, in one Rune reading, a sweet older lady had Fehu Reversed in her Root Chakra position. That was followed by Othila in her Sacral Chakra, Mannez in her Solar Plexus Chakra, Algiz in her Heart Chakra, Eihwaz in her Throat Chakra, Jera in her Third Eye Chakra and Isa in her Crown Chakra.

What this was showing was that she had been given as a foundational energy the ability to both create value and to deeply value herself (represented by Fehu). Because of early conditioning, this strong energy was turned around, creating a belief that she had to always have the short end of the stick, always be last, always take less.

That belief in the Root Chakra shifted the energies of the other Chakras. Othila in the Sacral Chakra deepened the sense of isolation and separation from the good things in life while reinforcing the belief that she had "inherited" a family pattern that demanded that she demean herself.

Mannez in the Solar Plexus Chakra urged her to come into alignment with herself, her womanhood, her humanity. Algiz in the Heart Chakra indicated a defensive or protective attitude around what she was willing to share and to accept from others. Can you see how this created even more of a sense of isolation?

Eihwaz in the Throat Chakra strengthened the idea that a defensive posture was necessary for interacting with the world. In this instance, the energy of Eihwaz also indicated a reluctance to speak her truth, again, reinforcing the belief that it was somehow wrong for her to believe in or value herself.

This created a sense of waiting, perhaps even needing to have her insights and intuitive observances validated by others before she could trust her own inner thoughts (Jera), which led to both the urging for deep meditation to correct this imbalance or a total standstill of energy (Isa) in her Crown Chakra.

Can you see how, by turning around the energy of the Root Chakra Rune, Fehu, she could have transformed the energy of her life?

If Fehu appeared upright in her Root, she would deeply value herself, shifting the interpretation of Othila in the Sacral Chakra to more of a confidence that she would find ways to "inherit" abundance and happiness in her life. This in turn would bring out the self-confident aspects of Mannez in the Solar Plexus, a healthy sense of personal boundaries through Algiz in the Heart Chakra, a sense of expertise and experience through Eihwaz in the Throat Chakra, an impeccable sense of timing through Jera in the Third Eye Chakra and a deep sense of groundedness and calm through Isa in the Crown Chakra.

It's also possible that once the energy of Fehu was set upright that other Runes would appear in the other Chakras, but you can see how shifting the energy of one Rune in one Chakra not only shifts the basic life energy but also informs the energies around the other major Chakras.

As you can see by now, the more you study Runes, the more aspects you'll learn that are covered by the energy governing each Rune. How deep you go into each aspect covered by the Runes is up to you. The main issue is to benefit yourself or the seeker. To do the most good, keep a balance.

When considering the Chakric aspects of a Rune cast, tie the Chakra color and energy into the overall theme and sub-themes of the Rune reading. For example, if the Rune cast contains Runes that are predominantly yellow, adding information about the Solar Plexus Chakra would be indicated.

This information would validate and strengthen the information contained in the Runic messages, giving an extra ray of clarity to the Rune reading.

If the Rune cast contains several colors, this can indicate that several Chakras need attention or are in play in the current life path. It can also be helpful to look for common themes in the different Chakra energies to focus on the main issues needing to be addressed.

If the main focus of the Rune Cast is a health issue, pay special attention to the areas of the body governed by the Chakras indicated in the Runes that appear in the cast.

In the case of several Chakra colors appearing in a Rune cast, instead of giving comprehensive information on each Chakra, consider the main energetic theme or themes of the reading and tie in the bits of Chakric information that will strengthen and validate the overall message.

In addition to the thematic messages contained in the Chakras, the Chakra system holds vibrational energies like musical tones of the music scale. There are quartz crystal bowls available that resonate with a Chakra and play the corresponding note. Following is a table that contains the colors, locations, main energetic concerns, glands and musical notes associated with each Chakra:

Violet: Crown Chakra--spiritual influence, enlightenment
Gland: Pineal
Musical note: B

Indigo: Third Eye Chakra—Thought, intuition, imagination,
psychic vision
Gland: Pituitary
Musical note: A

Blue: Throat Chakra—Communication, self-expression, ideas
Gland: Thyroid
Musical note: G

Green: Heart Chakra—Love, compassion, renewal of spirit
Gland: Thymus
Musical note: F

Yellow: Solar Plexus Chakra—Personal power, influence, the will
Gland: Pancreas
Musical note: E

Orange: Sacral Chakra—Strength, emotion, creativity, sexuality
Gland: Ovaries in women/testes in men
Musical note: D

Red: Root Chakra—grounding, instinct, security, survival
Gland: Adrenal cortex
Musical note: C

On the following pages, each of the seven major
Chakras is discussed in more detail.

1ˢᵗ Chakra: Muladhara = "Root" or "Support"

Color: Red, black

Runes: Fehu, Thurisaz, Raido, Kano, Eihwaz, Teiwaz, Mannez, Perth, Nauthiz, Isa

Spirit Animal: Mole

Purposes: Kinesthetic feelings, movement, survival, physical needs, material existence, strength

Spiritual Lesson: Material world lessons

Physical Dysfunctions: Lower back pain, sciatica, varicose veins, rectal tumors, depression, immune related disorders, osteoarthritis

Emotional Dysfunction: Mental lethargy; unable to arrive at stillness

Mental & Emotional Issues: Survival, self-esteem, social order, security

Family Info Stored in Root Chakra: Familial beliefs, superstitions, loyalty, instincts, physical pleasure or pain, touch

Area of Body Governed: Spinal column, kidneys, legs, feet, rectum, immune system

Glandular Connection: Adrenal glands, bladder, genitals, spine

Sense: Smell

Astrological Sign: Capricorn

Ruling Planet: Saturn

Musical Note: Middle C

Gemstones: Hematite, black tourmaline, onyx, garnet, red jasper, bloodstone, any red stone

Essential Oils: Cedarwood, patchouli, myrrh, cypress, vetiver, clove, rosemary

Flower essences: Corn, clematis, rosemary, sweet chestnut, rockrose

Foods to nurture Root Chakra: Root vegetables, carrots, potatoes, parsnips, radishes, beets, onions, garlic

Protein-rich Foods: Eggs, meat, beans tofu, soy products, peanut butter

Spices: Horseradish, hot paprika, chives, cayenne

Exercises for the Root Chakra: Stamping the feet, marching, doing squats

Affirmations: I have a right to express myself and manifest my dreams.

I can risk doing what I feel is right.

I trust in the power of life.

I feel at home in my body.

I am sustained and nourished by nature.

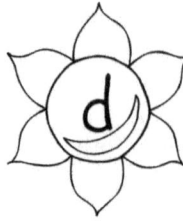

2nd Chakra: Sacral or sexual Chakra. Sanskrit name = Svadhisthana; "Sacred home of the self" or "Sweetness."

Color: Orange

Runes: There are no Runes associated with orange color, so the Runes associated with the Root Chakra can be used to indicate issues with both the Root and the Sacral Chakras.

Those Runes are:

Fehu, Thurisaz, Raido, Kano, Eihwaz, Teiwaz, Mannez

Spirit Animal: Badger

Purposes: Emotional balance, sexuality, change, pleasure

Spiritual Lessons: Creativity, manifestation, honoring relationships, learning to "let go"

Physical dysfunctions: Low back pain, sciatica, ob/gyn problems, pelvic pain, libido, urinary problems

Emotional dysfunctions: Unbalanced sex drive, feelings of isolation

Mental & Emotional Issues: Blame, guilt, money, sex, power, control, creativity, morality

Information Stored Inside 2nd Chakra: Duality, magnetism, controlling patterns, emotional feelings (joy, anger, fear, etc.)

Area of Body Governed: Sexual organs, stomach, upper intestines, liver, gallbladder, kidney, pancreas, adrenal glands, spleen, middle spine, bladder

Glandular Connection: Reproductive organs, urogenital system, kidneys, gonads, legs

Sense: Taste

Astrological Signs: Cancer, Scorpio

Ruling Planet: Pluto

Musical Note: D

Gemstones: Citrine, carnelian, moonstone, orange tourmaline

Essential Oils: Jasmine, patchouli, rose, sandalwood, myrrh, vanilla

Flower Essences: Indian paintbrush, lady's slipper, hibiscus, oak, olive, pine

Foods to nourish the Sacral Chakra: Sweet fruits, melons, mangos, strawberries, passion fruit, oranges, coconut, etc. Honey, nuts

Spices: Cinnamon, vanilla, carob, sweet paprika, sesame seeds, caraway seeds

Exercises: Pelvic thrusts, circular pelvic motions like belly dancing

Affirmations: I allow pleasure sweetness and sensuality into my life.

I release my negative attitudes which block my experience of pleasure.

I enjoy life with all of my senses.

I give my creativity and joy in living free rein.

I lovingly accept my body and my sensuality.

3rd Chakra: Solar Plexus or Manipura, which means "inner sun," "seat of the soul" or "luscious gem".

Color: Yellow

Runes: Inguz, Othila

Spirit Animal: Bear

Purposes: Mental understanding or emotional life, personal power, self will, transformation, wholeness

Spiritual Lesson: Acceptance of your place in the life stream (self-love)

Physical Dysfunctions: Stomach ulcers, intestinal tumors, diabetes, pancreatitis, indigestion, anorexia/bulimia, hepatitis, cirrhosis, adrenal imbalances, arthritis, colon diseases, chronic fatigue, allergies

Emotional Dysfunctions: Oversensitive to criticism, need to be in control, low self-esteem

Mental & Emotional Issues: Self-esteem, fear of rejection, oversensitivity to criticism, self-image fears, fears of our secrets being found out, indecisiveness

Information Stored in the 3rd Chakra: Personal power, personality, consciousness of self within the Universe (sense of belonging), knowing

Area of Body Governed: Upper abdomen, umbilicus to ribcage, liver, gallbladder, middle spine, spleen, kidney, adrenals, small intestines, stomach

Glandular Connection: Stomach, liver, gallbladder, pancreas, solar plexus

Sense: Sight

Astrological Sign: Aries, Leo

Ruling Planet: Mars, Sun

Musical Note: E

Gemstones: Sunstone, citrine, jasper, golden topaz, yellow tourmaline, amber

Essential Oils: Ylang ylang, lemongrass, peppermint, juniper, lemon, vetiver

Flower Essences: impatiens, scleranthus, and hornbeam

Foods to Nourish the Solar Plexus Chakra: Granola, grains, pastas, bread, cereal, rices, flax seed, sunflower seeds

Dairy: Milk, cheeses, yogurt

Spices: ginger, mints, Melissa, chamomile, turmeric, cumin, fennel

Exercises for the Solar Plexus Chakra: Dancing (twist, hula hoop, belly dancing)

Affirmations: I am worthy of my own self love.

I am worth my weight in gold.

I let my feelings run freely and trust my spontaneous decisions.

I use my inner strength to make the world a better place.

Through the power of my will, I can reach any goal.

4th Chakra: Heart Chakra, Anahata = "unstuck" or "unbeaten"

Colors: Green, pink

Runes: Uruz, Berkana, Laguz

Spirit Animal: Wolf

Purposes: Emotional empowerment, love, relationships, compassion, endurance

Spiritual Lesson: Forgiveness, unconditional love, letting go, trust, compassion

Physical Dysfunctions: Heart conditions, asthma, lung & breast cancers, thoracic spine, pneumonia, upper back, shoulder problems, high blood pressure

Emotional Dysfunctions: Fear about betrayal, co-dependent, melancholic

Mental & Emotional Issues: Love, compassion, confidence, inspiration, hope, despair, hate, envy, fear, jealousy, anger, generosity

Information Stored in the Heart Charka: Connections or "heart strings" to those we love

Area of Body Governed: Heart, circulatory system, blood, lungs, ribcage, diaphragm, thymus, breasts, esophagus, shoulders, arms, hands

Glandular Connection: Heart, lungs, circulation, thymus gland

Sense: Touch

Astrological Sign: Libra, Taurus

Ruling Planet: Venus

Musical Note: F

Gemstones: Rose Quartz, adventurine, malachite, emerald

Essential Oils: Pine, spruce, bergamot, rose, jasmine

Flower Essences: Holly, poppy, California wild rose, red chestnut, willow, chicory

Foods: Leafy vegetables, spinach, kale, dandelion greens. Air vegetables: broccoli, cauliflower, cabbage, celery, squash, etc.

Liquids: Green tea

Spices: Basil, sage, thyme, cilantro, parsley

Exercises: Push ups, swimming (breast stroke), hugging yourself

Affirmations: I open myself to the healing powers of love.

My heart is open to giving and receiving love.

I lovingly accept myself – as I am.

I give and receive with an open heart and bind myself to all living beings.

5th Chakra: Throat Chakra—Vishuddha = "purification"

Color: Blue

Runes: Ansuz, Gebo, Wunjo, Hagalaz, Jera, Dagaz, Odin

Spirit Animal: Personal Power Animal

Purposes: Learning to take responsibility for one's own needs

Communication: Self-expression, sound & hearing

Spiritual Lesson: Confession, surrender personal will over to Divine will, faith, truthfulness over deceit

Physical Dysfunctions: Sore throat, mouth ulcers, scoliosis, swollen glands, thyroid dysfunctions, laryngitis, voice problems, gum or tooth problems, TMJ

Emotional dysfunctions: Perfectionism, inability to express emotions, blocked creativity

Mental & Emotional Issues: Personal expression, creativity, addiction, criticism, faith, decision making (choices), will, lack of authority

Information stored in Throat Chakra: Self-knowledge, truth, attitudes, hearing, taste, smell

Area of Body Governed: Throat, thyroid, trachea, neck, vertebrae, mouth, teeth, gums, esophagus, parathyroid, thalamus

Glandular Connection: Throat, thyroid gland, upper lungs and arms, digestive tract

Sense: Hearing

Astrological Sign: Gemini, Virgo

Ruling Planet: Mercury

Musical Note: G

Gemstones: Chrysocola, lapis, blue opal

Essential Oils: Chamomile, myrrh, lavender, sandalwood, camphor

Flower Essences: Cosmos, trumpet vine, larch, mimulus, agrimony, cerato

Foods: Liquids, water, fruit juices, herbal teas, tart or tangy fruits, lemons, limes, grapefruits, kiwi, tree fruits, apple, pear, cherry, plums, peaches, apricots

Spices: Salt, lemon grass

Exercises: Gargling with salt water, singing, screaming

Affirmations: I am confident in the healing power of love to open my throat for greater self expression.

I speak from the heart and let the truth be my guide.

I use the power of words to make the world a better place.

Every day it becomes easier to express what I think and feel.

6th Chakra: Third Eye: Anja = "perception"

Color: Indigo blue

Runes: Ansuz, Gebo, Dagaz, Odin

Spirit Animal: Mountain Lion

Purposes: Action of ideas, insight, mind development, psychic intuition, wisdom

Spiritual Lesson: Understanding, reality check point, detachment, open mind, imagination

Physical Dysfunctions: Brain tumors, strokes, blindness, deafness, seizures, learning disabilities, spinal dysfunctions, hallucinations,

Mental & Emotional Issues: Fear of truth, discipline, judgment, evaluation, emotional intelligence, concept of reality, confusion

Information Stored in the 3rd Eye Chakra: Seeing clear picture, wisdom, intuition, mental facilities, intellect

Area of Body Governed: Brain, neurological system, ears, eyes, nose, pituitary, pineal glands

Glandular Connection: Lower brain, left eye, nose, spine, ears, pituitary gland

Sense: 6th sense, transcendental awareness

Astrological Sign: Sagittarius, Pisces

Ruling Planet: Neptune, Jupiter

Musical Note: A

Gemstones: Purple fluorite, sugalite, lapis, amethyst, sodalite, kyanite

Essential Oils: Geranium, lavender, juniper, clarysage, sandalwood, rosemary

Flower Essences: Wild oat, Queen Anne's lace, madia, crabapple, vine, walnut

Foods: Dark bluish fruits: blueberries, red grapes, blackberries, raspberries

Liquids: Red wines, grape juice

Spices: Poppy seed, mugwort

Exercises: Visualization, remote viewing, lucid dreaming

Affirmations: I rethink all negative thoughts about myself and others and change it to positive energy.

I am in touch with my inner light.

I let my fantasy run free.

I listen to my inner voice.

I look inward and recognize what is essential.

7th Chakra: Crown Chakra—Sahasrara=”Crown” or “Thousandfold”

Colors: Purple, white, gold

Runes: Algiz, Solwelu, Ehwaz

Spirit Animal: Eagle

Purposes: Intuitive knowing, connection to one's spirituality, integration of the whole, where the soul enters the body at birth and leaves the body at death, enlightenment, Divine self, fulfillment, Divine wisdom and understanding, cosmic energy

Spiritual Lesson: Spirituality, living in the NOW

Physical Dysfunctions: Mystical depression, diseases of the muscular system, skeletal system and skin, chronic exhaustion not associated with physical ailments, sensitivity to light, sound, environment, epilepsy, Alzheimer's

Emotional Dysfunctions: Depression, obsessive thinking, confusion

Mental & Emotional Issues: Discovery of the Divine, lack of purpose, loss of meaning or identity, trust, selflessness, humanitarianism, ability to see the bigger picture in the life stream, devotion, inspiration, values, ethics

Information Stored in Crown Chakra: Duality, magnetism, controlling patterns, emotional feelings (joy, anger, fear)

Area of Body Governed: Top center of the head, midline above the ears

Glandular Connection: Upper brain, right eye, pineal gland

Sense: Cosmic awareness

Astrological Sign: Aquarius

Ruling Planet: Uranus

Musical Note: B

Gemstones: Amber, diamond, moldavite, clear quartz, snow quartz, chevron, amethyst

Essential Oils: Lavender, frankincense, rosewood, elemi, clarysage

Flower Essences: Lotus, angelica, star tulip, wild rose, white chestnut

Foods: Air/fasting/detoxing

Incense & Smudging Herbs: Sage, copal, myrrh, frankincense and juniper (ritually inhaled through the nostrils or smoked for purification purposes)

Exercises: Prayer, meditation

Affirmations: I am divinely protected and guided.

I am fully aware – in my body, thoughts, and feelings.

The essence of my being is light and peace.

I open myself to the infinite power of God.

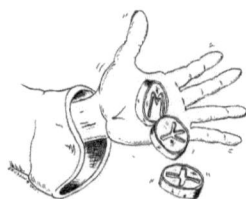

Incorporating Chakric Information in a Rune Cast

Incorporating Chakric themes and information in a Rune cast is done in the same way as considering the energetic themes of the Runes themselves.

For example, if you choose a three-Rune cast and draw Perth, Fehu and Dagaz, you have drawn three colors as well: Red, black and blue. Since the Root Chakra is associated with red and black, and the Throat and Third Eye Chakras are associated with blue, you can suggest that the seeker think about speaking his truth so that he can attain a balance between his sense of being grounded in this world and his overall place in the Universe.

This simple statement ties in the main energetic themes of the Root, Throat and Third Eye Chakras. This can open up a discussion about how the seeker can speak his truth, what it means to him to be grounded in general and in the world and what he feels is his place in the Universe.

You can draw upon any information contained in the Chakra energy as well as the thematic energy of the Runes. You might want to include information about the animal guide, emotional ties or include crystals in your Rune reading.

If you or your seeker would like a Rune cast in order to focus on Chakric issues, you can consider using a Rune cast specifically designed to focus on Chakric energy. To do that you can hold the Rune pouch and ask the Runes to share insight into the Chakra or Chakras the seeker needs to focus on. Then draw one or several Runes, discussing the Chakric issues and themes of each.

You may also choose to share a Chakric Rune cast in a specific pattern.

One possible Chakric Rune cast would be the seven-Rune cast that is outlined below.

The Runes are to be placed bottom to top. Each Rune represents a Chakra position, though the Rune pulled for that position might not correspond directly to the Chakra. For example, if the Rune Thurisaz is in the Root Chakra (first) position that is also a Root Chakra Rune, which strengthens the messages received for the Root Chakra. But if Gebo is in the Root Chakra position, since it is a Throat/Third Eye Chakra, that could indicate more grounding is needed in the Throat and/or Third Eye Chakras.

As stated before, the energetic connections will give your seekers the most useful and practical information so that the energy of the Runes can be incorporated into everyday life.

Chakric Rune Cast
Rune 1 (bottom position): Root Chakra
Rune 2: Sacral Chakra
Rune 3: Solar Plexus Chakra
Rune 4: Heart Chakra
Rune 5: Throat Chakra
Rune 6: Third Eye Chakra
Rune 7: Crown Chakra

Sample Chakra Rune Reading:

Rune 1: Root Chakra

Raido, Rune of Communication. This Rune in the Root position indicates that a strong energetic flow in the areas of communication is available for you to utilize as needed in Chakras that are partially blocked. That the Rune of Communication has showed up in your Root Chakra indicates that this Chakra is open and ready to send grounding energy where needed.

Rune 2: Sacral Chakra

Jera, Rune of the Cycles of the Natural Order

Jera in the Sacral position indicates that you may be putting the needs of others before your own needs and/or waiting to develop your own ideas until someone else validates you. The aspect of Jera that pertains to the Sacral Chakra is that of waiting. Jera promises that the things you create and invent are based on solid ideas and will create a good harvest, providing you actually get down to business and create them.

Call on the Root Chakra energy to ground your Sacral Chaka to remove any false beliefs that putting yourself, your needs, your passions, ideas and desires last is noble or necessary. The more deeply you trust yourself the more at peace you will be.

Rune 3: Solar Plexus Chakra

Wunjo, Rune of Joy. The Rune that appears in the Solar Plexus Chakra area can indicate a major energetic theme of your life. This means that a Rune in this position can be considered a Heart Rune because the energy around the Solar Plexus Chakra indicates your deepest sense of being. This is because the Solar Plexus Chakra is the nexus point of our ideas about who we are and what we're all about.

The energy of the Solar Plexus Chakra can be a deeply-held secret, especially when the energies surrounding other Chakras indicate that you have a habit of keeping your feelings and desires a secret. One of the challenges that arises when you keep your deepest inner motives secret from others is that you can end up keeping them secret from yourself as well.

Given the hesitation and sense of waiting indicated by Jera in the Sacral position, the thread of Joy may be at least partly hidden from you. Sometimes it can seem fun to keep secrets, especially if the joy of life itself wasn't a theme in our childhood lives. This may be the case here. To derive benefit from this Rune, again, send some of the strong grounding communication energy of Raido from the Root to the Solar Plexus Chakra, giving yourself permission to own the joy you feel at just being alive.

Rune 4: Heart Chakra

Gebo, Rune of Partnership. Gebo in the Heart position speaks of the desire for complete and balanced partnerships of all kinds, be they friendship, marriage, parenting, or business relationships. The energy behind deep desire for equality is revealed through the other Runes in this spread: Raido, that shows a foundation in communication, Gebo, indicating patience as well as a reticent attitude about your ability to bring things into being, (would feel more comfortable bringing out the ideas and energies of others) and Wunjo, the deeply hidden secret that at the core of who you perceive yourself to be, there is a joy in life itself that has often been difficult to openly express.

To balance the first four Chakras, take a good look at the wonderful energetic elements that are expressed in your life each day.

Rune 5: Throat Chakra

Isa, Rune of the Meditative Mind. Isa in the Throat position in relation to the other Runes in this spread, encompasses both ends of the spectrum of the energy surrounding what is sometimes called the Stillness Rune.

Isa can indicate moments when not much is moving in our lives, which is one end of the spectrum, but those moments of stillness also give us the opportunity to dive deeply into the mindset of meditation and contemplation. Isa in the Throat Chakra position also indicates a reluctance to speak your deep inner truth, whether because you aren't sure that there really is truth deep inside of you or perhaps because you have been taught over and over that your own individuality is invalid.

Consider the earlier Runes in this spread to think through the issue or issues that has you stopped.

Rune 6: Third Eye Chakra

Fehu, Rune of Possessions, Reversed. Having Fehu Reversed in the Third Eye position can strengthen the iciness, stagnation and/or need for deeper introspection indicated by Isa at the Throat Chakra. Fehu is concerned with having plenty of what you need and in this spread the indication is that the greatest need is for self-discovery and a deeper sense of self-trust.

Another area to consider is how well grounded you are in your sense of acceptance and comfort at just being you. There is a possibility that your bottom four Chakras are not communicating effectively with your top three Chakras. As mentioned before, send communication from the Root Chakra up through all the rest of your Chakras, to balance and strengthen your system.

Remember, your greatest wealth is the development of yourself.

Rune 7: Crown Chakra

Algiz, Rune of Protection, Reversed. It's easy to see the progression of energy in this Rune cast. There is good communication at the Root, which leads to a harvest, albeit a reluctant one at times, at the Sacral Chakra. But since joy in the Solar Plexus Chakra and the longing for equal and balanced partnership in the Heart Chakra are hidden, the communication breaks down beginning at the Throat Chakra.

I hope you can see that a lack of openness in expressing major life energies like the creation of ideas and of joy leads to less and less communication in the energy pathways of the body/mind/spirit. Without a proper foundation, it's no wonder that there is a feeling of lack of connection in the Crown Chakra.

Chapter 8:
Choosing Runes

Runes can be carved into bone, stone, wood. I've even seen plastic Runes and Rune cards. Since a main theme of Rune reading is intuitive knowledge, the intent and the energetic connection with the Runes is more important than the material from which they are made.

That said, anyone wishing to begin reading Runes would be wise to carefully consider all options available. Pay attention to what draws you to a Rune set, whether the set is made of wood, stone or paper. Allow your intuition to lead you to the set that is right for you.

I resonate well with amethyst and am a Crystal Reiki Master so I chose a set of amethyst Runes. My husband is highly creative and individualistic, so he created his own set of Runes. He carved his set of Runes from fossil mammoth ivory. By adding his creative energy to the overall energetic intent of the Runes to help and guide, he made a very deep connection to his highly original set of Runes.

I wasn't drawn to the wooden Runes I've seen in some crystal or magic shops, but I've created my own special wooden Runes using some of the sacred woods on our property. Woods like laurel, cedar, willow, hawthorn, holly or apple have wonderful energetic properties that lend themselves well to Rune casting.

If you choose to create a set of Runes for yourself using wood from your property, you can buy a wood burning kit to burn the symbols into the wood, use a dremel to carve the symbols, or paint or draw the symbols on the wood.

Working with the various woods on my property helped me see the importance of not being a materials snob, since again it is the intent and the interplay between reader, seeker, Runes and Universe that facilitates the Universal wisdom that flows around us all, not the material, that is the most important aspect.

By the way, the Runic graffiti at the beginning of this chapter spells out "this one."

As with the other Runic graffiti messages I've used, this one also contains an appropriate message for choosing Runes. Thurisaz (the "th") reminds us to take our time and consider carefully as we choose the Runes or other energetic tools we will work with. Isa (the "I") reminds us to take a moment to commune deeply with the Runes before we use them. Sowelu (the "S") reminds us that our goal in using Runes or other energetic tools is to bring us to a place of wholeness.

Othila (the "O" in "One") reminds us that it's a blessing to obtain and learn to use energetic tools, Nauthiz (the "N") reminds us that using energetic tools can help us be more self-reliant and Ehwaz (the "E") reminds us not to think we know all there is to know about the Runes. As long as we keep moving forward in our knowledge of the Runes, they will keep teaching us on deeper and deeper levels.

Chapter 9:
How to Read Runes

Ted J. Kaptchuk, O.M.D. said, "This deeper layer of a person, usually involving the Spirit, can sometimes reveal the clearest delineation of a pattern."[15]

Since patterns are what we are concerned with when reading the Runes, I hope you can see how important Runic interpretations can be to all aspects of life.

In reading Runes, I've found it helpful to remember several things:

Look for patterns within patterns. The patterns of each cast are cycles within cycles. A major pattern of energy is shown, pointing to the roots of the seeker's present issues. Embedded in this general pattern are smaller patterns that can pinpoint energetic patterns in everyday life—habits that the person may not be aware are affecting their desired outcome. In general, major energetic patterns indicate major life issues, much as the Major Arcana of the Tarot. Minor patterns indicate everyday challenges, smaller energetic patterns that are similar to the Minor Arcana of the Tarot.

---

[15] Kaptchuk, Ted J., The Web That Has No Weaver, p. 193.

For example, if a seeker's present energetic pattern is one of change, often the life cycle pattern will indicate where they are in the present energetic pattern. Have they just begun to make changes or have they been in the process of change for a long time?

Look also for the indications of cycles. Life cycles have a definite beginning and ending. If a seeker is exhausted by weathering many changes, the present energy pattern may show the need for patience and perseverance. The life cycle pattern embedded in the overall pattern may show that the cycle of constant change is nearing its end, giving the hope and perspective needed to complete the cycle.

Compare the energetic signatures of the Runes. For example, if the Growth Rune, Berkana, and the Harvest Rune, Gera, show up in the same pattern, this indicates an overall theme of growth in the seeker's life. Since both Berkana and Gera contain an element of patience this can indicate the need for patience in the endeavor or concern the seeker has asked about. These Runes are also growth Runes, which can indicate quicker growth. In other cases, especially if a growth Rune is in the challenge position, the growth may be fast enough to be stressful. Growth can also indicate pregnancy, business or inner growth—the 'growth of a will' as Ralph H. Blum puts it.[16]

Consider the subtle shifting of meaning through Runic combinations. For example, if the Growth Rune, Berkana appears with the Initiation Rune, Perth, the seeker may be being asked to take an active role in the development of new ideas or projects.

The ultimate message of the Runes always points to developing a deeper relationship with the self. From the Self Rune, Mannez, the first of the Runes, to Odin, the Blank Rune, last of the Runes and a reminder that the Self is limitless, the main goal of Rune readings is to create a deep,

---

[16] The Book of Runes, Ralph H. Blum, page 113.

conscious connection of the self to the Higher Self. As Tony Willis writes in Discover Runes, the word 'rune' comes from a root meaning 'a secret' and 'to whisper' and 'a mystery', depending on the source you refer to.[17] All of these definitions remind us that when we seek the counsel of the Runes, we are delving into our own deepest selves.

The motivation of the reader is not to prove that the reader is a powerful psychic or to show insightful or connected to the Universe she or he is. The motivation is to be an open channel, a detached Observer of the sacred connection between seeker and Universe. Remember that the Runes themselves show only as much of themselves as is necessary to help the seeker connect to the Universe.

Look for a moving pattern. If using the Runic Cross pattern, for example, the underlying energy shows a main energy that is giving life to the overall pattern. This is a changing, evolving pattern, as the Odin or Blank Rune reminds us, the lessons of karma are the sum total of our actions in this lifetime—and karma shifts and evolves as we shift and evolve.

---

[17] Willis, Tony. *Discover Runes: Understanding and Using the Power of Runes*, p. 17.

Chapter 10: Rune Polarities:
Masculine, Feminine and Balance Runes

Many people think most of the Runes are masculine in nature, but if you look at their meanings from an energetic standpoint, the number of individuating masculine or Sun Runes (yang) and intuitive feminine or Moon Runes (yin) is more balanced.

Our Runic graffiti above speaks to the humanity inherent in the Runes. The word above is "human."

The meanings underlie the deepest meaning of the archetypal symbols represented by Runic symbols.

Hagalaz (the "H") speaks to the challenges of living a human life, as well as how often those challenges bring out the best in us, by pushing us to invent new ways to achieve freedom and liberation.

Uruz (the "U") speaks to the strength of character and integrity needed to develop balanced inner and outer strength.

Mannez (the "M") speaks to the theme of what it means to be human, including the act of being in balance as a unique self and as a part of a larger whole.

Algiz (the "A") reminds us to listen well on all levels of our lives: physically, intuitively and psychically, and to balance our listening with our own inner wisdom.

Nauthiz (the "N") urges us to become self-reliant and to experience life with great patience.

So you can see that by asking the Runes to spell the word "human" in our current language, the messages they hold for us still ring true. And, hopefully, you can also see the balance in the energy contained in the Runes.

I've determined which Runes are masculine and which are feminine by intuiting which Runes ask the seeker to use masculine energy to dare to stand apart from the crowd and which Runes challenge the seeker to use feminine energy to listen to intuition.

Since many of the Runes are balanced in their feminine and masculine aspects, I feel many Runes are neutral or what I like to call Runes of Balance. Runes of Balance incorporate both masculine and feminine energies.

I've listed the Masculine, Feminine and Runes of Balance below. A more detailed description of each Rune is included in chapter 13. As you'll see, there are more Runes of Balance than Masculine or Feminine Runes.

For this description I've used traditional identifiers for each Rune. As you will see in the detailed description, I've also created an energetic title for each Rune.

Masculine Runes:

As our Runic graffiti shows, masculine Runes have a lot of "he" or sun energy. Sun energy is the energy of individuation—of not being afraid to stand up and be noticed. That can both cause disruption to others as we dare to stand out from the crowd and create a catalyst for change, as the first Rune, Hagalaz shows. The second Rune, Ehwaz, contains the energy of the sun and of the steady forward progress that comes with daring to create change.

Othila: Rune of Separation, or Rune of Energetic Fences. Since separation involves individuation, Othila is a masculine Rune.

Uruz: Rune of Strength and Empowerment. Brute strength is at the heart of Uruz, which is shaped like the horns of an aurochs, or wild ox, making Uruz a masculine Rune.

Algiz: Rune of Protection and Personal Space. Shaped like a deer antler, Algiz protects by calling on the inner Spiritual Warrior, so is masculine in nature.

Teiwaz: The Warrior Rune, or Rune of the Divinity in Humanity. Teiwaz holds the energy of being willing and able to stand up for what is important in life, to use masculine energy to stand out from the crowd.

Ehwaz: Rune of Movement and Unbreakable Bond. Ehwaz holds the masculine energies of steady forward movement, and was developed to depict the path of the sun across the sky.

Dagaz: Rune of Breakthrough and Transformation. Dagaz holds the masculine energy of daylight, success and completion.

Feminine Runes:

Our Runic graffiti, spelling the word, "she" shows that the feminine can also be strong and lead others into the light, represented by Sowelu (the "s"). And when the feminine dares to shine, that also can challenge relationships, but lead to higher levels of freedom and liberation, represented by Hagalaz (the "h"). I chose our other "E" Rune, Eihwaz, to complete this word, to speak of the wisdom of the feminine as well as the ability to wisely choose life's battles.

Inguz: Rune of Fertility and the Beacon of Light. Fertility is a feminine trait, making Inguz a feminine Rune.

Eihwaz: Rune of Defense and Experience. I place Eihwaz among the Feminine Runes because a nuance of this Rune is aversive or strategic skills rather than strength alone.

Wunjo: Rune of Joy and Fellowship. Wunjo hold the feminine energies of harmony that brings joy and of balance and the bearing of fruit.

Gera: Rune of Harvest and Natural Cycles. Gera holds the feminine energies of harvest, reaping the benefits of a life path that is well and gently tended.

Berkana: Rune of Growth and Rising Vibrations. Berkana holds the feminine energies of creating new growth and of caring for life in a compassionate way.

Laguz: Rune of Flow and Abundant Life Force. As a water Rune, Laguz holds the feminine energies of receptivity, the ability to be compassionate and those that that connect us to the intuition.

Runes of Balance:

I chose the word "we" for the Runes of Balance. When humanity works together for the benefit of all, the result is great joy, represented by Wunjo (the "W"). This allows for true progress, both in society and in individual lives, represented by Ehwaz (the "E").

Mannez: Rune of the Self and of the Source. Since Mannez stands for both manhood and womanhood, I consider this a Rune of Balance.

Gebo: Rune of Partnership and Energetic Exchange. Since Gebo is concerned with equal and balanced partnership, it is neutral, a Rune of Balance.

Kano: Rune of Opening and Transforming Knowledge. Kano holds the masculine energy of creating new experiences and recognizing new opportunities when they come up, as well as the feminine energy of receptivity, making it a Rune of Balance.

Ansuz: Rune of Signals and the Divine Muse. Ansuz is a Rune of the God Loki so may seem masculine at first glance. But it is also a Rune that urges listening to the intuition, a feminine trait.

Perth: Rune of Initiation and Secrets. Perth is a Rune of Balance because while initiation often urges individuation, the mystery aspect of this Rune also challenges the seeker to listen to the intuition.

Nauthiz: Rune of Constraint and Self-Reliance. Nauthiz is concerned with the limitations we place on ourselves and seeing how those limitations hold wisdom. Fortitude is needed to look at the difficulties in our lives, and intuition is needed to see the benefits of and reasons for the difficulties, making this a Rune of Balance.

Fehu: Rune of Possessions and the Rising Spiral. Fehu contains the masculine energy of strong upward movement and the ability to follow through and create wealth. This Rune also holds the feminine energy of nourishment and asks the seeker to think through what means most in life, making Fehu a Rune of Balance.

Hagalz: Rune of Disruption and Deliberate Crisis. Hagalz is a Rune of Balance because it holds both the masculine energies of change and liberation but also holds the feminine energies of freedom and the challenge to look for deep inner motivation and meaning.

Raido: Rune of Journey and Expertise. Raido is a Rune of Balance because it contains the energy of the attunement of issues that have more than one side, of union and the rejoicing at the end of a journey.

Thurisaz: Rune of Energetic Gateways. Thurisaz is a Rune of Balance because it contains the masculine energy of the type of obstacles and snags that urge change and the feminine energy of being able to look at an imperfect life and bless it.

Isa: Rune of Stillness and the Contemplative Mind. Isa holds the feminine energies of gentleness and compassionate consideration and the masculine energies of the power to bring on a thaw and to bring into being a new path or a refreshed motion.

Sowelu: Rune of Wholeness, Immortality and Hope. Though Sowelu is a Sun Rune, it is also a Rune of Balance because its ultimate concern is that of wholeness. Wholeness requires balanced yin/yang or feminine/masculine energies.

Odin: The Blank Rune; Rune of Unlimited Potential. Odin holds the masculine energy of potential and of endings and the feminine energy of beginnings and of the ability to discern overall life patterns.

Freya

Chapter 11:
The Concept of Heart Runes

I've been aware of Runes since I noticed the man who would become my husband writing in Runes during college classes in the 1980s. That was his clever way of carving out a bit of private space to express his inner thoughts in a public setting.

Through many years of working with Runes, I've noticed that certain Runes would come up over and over again in my own castings as well as my husband's and in castings done for friends and others.

So I did an experiment. I placed my amethyst Runes in their velvet bag and sent an intention, which is a clear, focused, open-ended thought, requesting the Runes show me my heart Rune—the Rune that would show a major energetic theme running through my life as a whole.

Sowelu, the Sun Rune, a Rune that had shown up many times as my underlying energy, emerged from the bag.

Sowelu is important to me because it showed an overall life pattern. Though I've had my share, perhaps in some ways more than my share, of life challenges, my deliverance over and over again was to dare to stand out and be different on my path to becoming whole. My overall life focus as well was seeking out ways to become whole, so Sowelu was an excellent Heart Rune for me.

Now I remember Sowelu when life is challenging or difficult. This gives me perspective to see that though the present may be stressful, the overall theme of the sun's energy would pull me through in the end as it always had.

Finding Your Heart Rune

The most important aspect of seeking a Heart Rune is to recognize and accept the flow of energy that has been a hallmark of our particular life path. Ask the Universe to show you what energy has been foundational to your life, then let go of the intention and cast the Runes.

As I tested my Heart Runes casts on many others, in each case, the Rune cast indicated a major life theme. As such, the Heart Runes speak to the energy of Chi, the Lifeforce energy that flows through everyone and everything, linking us all as one.

Ted Kaptchuk, author of *The Web that Has No Weaver* said, "There is 'no place that does not have it, and no place it does not penetrate.'"[18]

Seeing our life issues in this respect can help us see that even the most challenging experiences have a purpose. Runes can help us to recognize the patterns and see the underlying purpose. The deepening of our understanding of our established patterns can facilitate a deeper and more complete understanding of ourselves.

---

[18] Ted Kaptuchuk, "The Web That Has No Weaver: Understanding Chinese Medicine", p. 47.

Chapter 12:
How to Give a Rune Reading

Giving a Rune reading is a sacred act. I've given general guidelines throughout this work but will also provide a list of things in this chapter for your convenience and continued enlightenment.

The Runic graffiti I've chosen for this chapter is the word "Read." Raido (the "R") reminds us of the importance of being open to change through various means of communication. Since there are two Runes that begin with "E," I had the choice of either Ehwaz (for motion) or Eihwaz (defense). I chose Eihwaz for the "E," since being well-informed helps us see more clearly so that we can sidestep snags and be aware of possible setbacks. Ansuz (the "A"), reminds us to listen to our inner wisdom before stepping out into the world and Dagaz (the "D") indicates that breakthroughs in our lives are possible when we listen well.

Before you begin

Calm your energy and center yourself. You can do this by taking a few deep breaths, meditating for a minute or so with the specific seeker in mind or simply sitting quietly with the Rune pouch in your palm.

Once you're centered and grounded, cup your Rune pouch in your palms and send a clear intent that you are invoking the energy of the Runes with respect and for the highest and greatest good of the person asking for insight.

This idea of centering and grounding, then connecting with respect to the energy behind the Runes is similar to the first and second pillars of Reiki. Reiki is an ancient Japanese method of communicating energetically with the body/mind/spirit to promote optimal health and balance. As a multi-level Reiki Master, the energetic qualities of the ancient hands-on energtic qualities of Reiki dovetail into my Rune readings.

In Reiki, the first pillar is to establish a connection between the Reiki Practitioner, the Universe and the person seeking Reiki. The second pillar is a moment of thanks for that connection. The third pillar is the Reiki treatment itself.[19]

You can prepare for a Rune reading in a similar way. Spend a few moments establishing a connection between yourself, the Runes, the Universe and the seeker's energy. We could call this the first pillar of Rune reading.

Next, spend a moment in gratitude for the indication or knowing that the energetic connection has been established. We could call this the second pillar of Rune reading.

Finally, approach the reading as an open channel, remaining present to the energies that come up and conveying the messages to the seeker that are contained in those energies without embellishing the messages with any aspects of your own ego energy.

The Reading

Once a strong connection is established, ask the seeker what he or she would like to learn. This can inform you as to what type of spread to use. The following chapter will

---

[19] Rand, William Lee. *Reiki: The Healing Touch*, D-1, D-2

show you various spreads from which you can choose. Use your intuition to guide you regarding which spread to use.

If the seeker has a single, straightforward question, you might choose to use a three-Rune spread for past, present and future, or to show insight into three aspects of the situation.

If the seeker wants to balance her energy, the Chakra Rune cast would be an appropriate choice. That cast contains one Rune for each of the seven major Chakra centers (for a detailed description of the Chakra Rune cast, see chapter 7).

If the seeker wishes to see a dominant energetic pattern in her life, you might choose the Runic Cross, with Runes for past, present, future, underlying energy, possible challenge and a possible outcome.

No Ego Needed

Remember, the energy behind the Runes respects free will and encourages the development of self-reliance, which is why the Runes aren't predictive tools. That's why I say "possible challenge" and "possible outcome."

You don't need to try to "fix" a difficult situation or provide any possible solutions. All you need do is share the energetic messages represented by the Runic symbols. As necessary, remind the seeker of the Universal Laws governing each symbol. This will help them to see that they aren't alone and that no matter what the circumstance, there are choices that can be made.

Look for Patterns

Like a weather forecast, a Rune reading shows one or more energetic patterns. Once the seeker is aware of the patterns he has set into motion by the choices he has made, he has the opportunity to shift his energy, thereby shifting the nature of the challenge and possibly changing the outcome.

Knowing that you won't be predicting anything for anyone challenges you to approach the Runes with an open mind and heart, as an open channel. If a seeker presses you to predict something for him, remain firm in the idea that each person establishes his own energetic patterns. Explain this to the seeker so that he has the opportunity to become more self-reliant.

Development of the Self

The main goal of Rune lore is the development, healing and balancing of the self. So when reading for yourself or a seeker, trust the Runic energy, the Universe and your own inner wisdom to bring out the themes and sub-themes that are relevant for that specific reading. In other words, don't worry about conveying every nuance of each Rune in the spread. Trust the messages that come through for you and for the seeker.

Remember that your intuitive or psychic abilities aren't being tested. It's your willingness to share the messages that come through from the Universe and your deep connection to the Universal truths that surpass human logic and laws that is most important.

Unclear Messages?

Sometimes the messages sent by the Runes don't provide a clear path for you or the seeker to see possible ways to shift the energy. In many ways this is the toughest challenge of trust, both for you and the seeker. Often this is because the situation is complex or difficult. In cases such as these, patience is a transformative tool. Even when the Runic messages don't provide as direct a path as the seeker would like, persevering in implementing the lessons with clear intent and patience is important.

An old saying goes, "The reward of patience is patience."

Sometimes, this is the truest message we can convey. Even, and actually especially, when the messages contained in the Runes are either unclear or contain elements that the seeker doesn't want to hear, time and patience are needed to think on the energetic patterns indicated and allow the meanings for the seeker's present life to become clear.

Yes, if you're reading for a fee, remaining true to the messages conveyed by the Runes without adding any fluff from your ego when those messages are unclear or unwanted could mean the seeker refuses to pay you. But remember the core energy of sharing Runic messages—that of being of the greatest service in sharing energetic messages with those who ask.

Some seekers may offer you far more than your reading price. Others may walk away shaking their heads, thinking you don't know what you're doing. That's the nature of energetic work.

And that's why the reward of patience is patience: nothing more, and nothing less.

Remember to have fun!

We're all on a journey together—the marvelous, challenging, sometimes daunting journey of life. Energetic tools like the Runes are here to guide and provide insight and perspective. Remember that we create our future in our present moments, not by seeking or following predictions.

Chapter 13:
Sample Rune Casts

The patterns of Rune casts are similar to those of other oracular tools. There are one, three, five and six Rune cast patterns that go by various names depending on the intent of the cast and the person or group that originated the cast.

Remember that the intent is the most important aspect of Rune casting. When determining how many Runes to cast, consider the complexity of your question or questions and your purpose in consulting the Runes.

The underlying intent of all Rune casts is contained in the Runic graffiti above. The word I spelled is "Cast".

Kano (the "C") stands for bringing light into a dark space.

Algiz (the "A") reminds us of the importance of being open to receiving messages from a bigger perspective than our own.

Sowelu (the "S") reminds us that we're seeking wholeness when we seek the wisdom of the Runic symbols.

Teiwaz (the "T") informs us that the inner warrior will guide us into a deeper sense of wisdom as well as a stronger and more balanced sense of self.

Upside-Down and Sideways Runes

If the Rune is cast upside down or Merkstave (sideways for Runes that have no Reverse), this doesn't simply mean the opposite of the Rune's upright interpretation, nor does it indicate a negative outcome. Runes are multi-dimensional. A Reversed or Merkstave Rune simply shows different aspects for you to consider.

Here are several methods for you to consider when casting Runes:

Using Runes Like a Pendulum

Just as there are many ways to cast Runes, there are many ways to use the Runes as well. For example, if you need immediate insight, use the Runes like a pendulum by focusing your intent on your need, sending that intent to the Runes and the Universe, and drawing a single Rune.

Glean as much insight as possible from that Rune. Remember that if you need more information or confirmation regarding your issue, you can repeat the above process until you have gained enough insight to move forward.

Three Rune Cast

If you would like an overview of the day's energy, a three-Rune cast that has existed for thousands of years is a good choice.

Relax your mind and send a clear thought to the Runes and to the Universe about the day ahead of you. Working right to left, draw three Runes from your Rune bag.

The first Rune gives an overview of the day ahead.

The second Rune indicates a challenge or challenges that you may face.

The third Rune shows actions you can take or an outcome that could appear.

The Three Rune Cast can be used for many issues. If you are making a tough decision, casting the Runes each day can show subtle shifts in energy. For some people, this may be like watching the scale every day in that the small increments of movement can feel frustrating.

If that sounds like you, wait a few days to check your progress.

Others benefit from being able to fine-tune the energy of the day so doing a Three-Rune Cast Daily can be helpful.

Five-Finger Rune Cast

Each hand has five fingers so it's not surprising that Runes, Tarot, Angel cards and other intuitive tools suggest using five of the tool to gain insight. I've named this spread the Five-Finger Rune Cast because it not only mirrors the major aspects of a seeker's present life, but also shows the complexity of our modern lives when so often, many options are available.

In a similar way to the *I Ching*, Runes have a mathematical aspect. Using five or more Runes increases the odds of any one set of Runes being drawn. This makes each Rune cast unique and individualistic.

As with other five spreads or casts, the Five-Rune Cast is drawn in descending order. Focus clearly and calmly on your intent and draw five Runes, one at a time. Place them one below the other.

Rune 1: The Thumb: gives perspective of the recent past.

Rune 2: The Index Finger: indicates the energy that is developing in the present.

Rune 3: The Middle Finger: indicates the foundational or grounding aspect of the energy that is pushing forward the present pattern.

Rune 4: Ring Finger: indicates a supporting energy that you can use to help you achieve your goal.

Rune 5: Pinky Finger: indicates a new situation that is emerging.

The word *emerging* is especially helpful for gaining perspective. If you draw Fehu as your fifth Rune, for example, and you don't receive a huge blessing on the day you cast the Runes, remember that as in the *I Ching*, the last Rune is part of an emerging pattern—one that has not yet completely formed.

The blessing of Fehu can also be energetic in nature, so the blessings that develop, while they may be physical, can also be blessings of deeper insight, clearer vision that will lead to an increased ability to welcome blessings into your life.

If you become discouraged or allow doubt to rise, that can shift your energy so that you move farther from prosperity. So you can see that the issue around Fehu isn't that you will definitely receive a physical blessing, but of the idea of what is a blessing in your life, and what isn't.

If you see prosperity as an emerging energy in your life, you can use the presence of Fehu as encouragement to increase your energy in that area and as an encouragement that you are moving down a strong energy path that will help you in the long run. Drawing Fehu as the fifth Rune can also indicate that your beliefs about prosperity are changing.

Here is a sample Five-Finger Rune Reading:

Rune 1: Thumb position: The past:

Gebo, Rune of Partnership. The ability to get along with people, come to an agreement, treat others fairly and be treated fairly yourself has often given you the advantage in interpersonal relationships. Gebo is a big "X" and this speaks to the grounded nature of your personality and how your grounded energy draws other like-minded people to you.

Rune 2: Index Finger position: Emerging energy of the present:

Nauthiz, Rune of Constraint and Need. Nauthiz was used as a signal to warn others of a disaster or a pressing need. This indicates a situation that is developing in which you will need to ask for help or assistance. The more quickly you recognize this and the more willing you are to reach out for help, the less restrictive this energy will be in your life.

Rune 3: Middle Finger position: Foundational Grounding Aspect:

Hagalaz: Rune of Disruption. This Rune pushes us to create ways to overcome, circumvent or solve the challenges that appear in our lives. Hagalaz indicates the need for a strong energetic push to bring change to your life and to the world. Combined with Gebo and Nauthiz, this indicates that the energy of partnership will help you to network and troubleshoot the emerging difficult situation, bringing energy to create new solutions or invent new ways of being that will bring you back to a place of grounding and centeredness.

Rune 4: Ring Finger position: Supporting Energy:

Ansuz, Rune of Messages from the Universe. This Rune indicates your willingness to listen to your inner wisdom and to the wisdom of the Universe. This reinforces the whole pattern by indicating that you will find a way to deal with the challenging situation that is forming.

Rune 5: Pinky Finger position: New Situation Emerging:

Gera: Rune of Harvest and Beneficial Outcome. This shows that you are taking the steps necessary to create a positive outcome in your situation. Just as a gardener must spend time pulling weeds to ensure a bountiful harvest, so the challenges that are forming in your life will help you to be more diligent and to find ways to make lemons into lemonade, so to speak.

The Runic Cross

The Runic Cross is similar to the Celtic Cross of the Tarot. It consists of six Runes, cast in a cross shape. The Runic Cross is also an ancient spread, one of the oldest in existence.

The six Runes are cast as follows:

Right to left:

Rune 1 indicates energy in the past (recent or distant or both, depending on the seeker's request)

Rune 2 indicates the energy present in life now.

Rune 3 indicates an emerging energy of the future.

Rune 4 is placed below Rune two, and indicates a strong thread of energy flowing through life, that is pushing the entire energy pattern forward.

Rune 5 is placed above Rune two and indicates a challenge that may be faced.

Rune 7 is placed above Rune five and indicates a new situation that is emerging.

Again, the last Rune cast is concerned with what is emerging. The final outcome may not be clear but there will be hints, clues to indicate what the developing energy may become. The more keenly you are able to see the emerging pattern, the easier it is to influence and guide the energy where you would like it to go, or to change direction to encourage new energy in your life.

You can see the pattern within the pattern of this cast. Rune three shows a future energetic pattern that is already beginning to form. Rune six shows a new situation that is emerging, but may not have yet developed to the point where it is recognizable. The Runes in these two positions often compliment each other. When they don't, they may be indicating two aspects of the concern that was brought, or two main energetic themes in your life.

It's helpful to see patterns developing in our lives because we're often too close to our own issues to pick up on the subtle changes until they manifest—sometimes in ways that we wish they wouldn't.

If more information is needed, a seventh Rune can be cast, sometimes called a confirmation Rune. The seventh Rune is cast to the side of the original spread, to indicate that it is separate from the main energy pattern. It is like the extended weather forecast, reaching out a bit farther and indicating other energy patterns that are affecting the pattern you are studying.

Here is a sample Runic Cross pattern reading:

Rune 1: Past

I drew Perth, which stands for Initiation. Perth is also called a Mystery Rune because it often is present at times when our lives are up in the air. That can feel disconcerting but what it really means is that there are many things in flux in our lives. Some things are in the process of changing and/or ending, other things are in the process of coming to light and/or forming/beginning. This Rune reminds us that we cannot control what is not yet in form. It challenges us to discover and learn to trust our Observer self. The Observer self watches without judgment, noting the progress of life events. Because of its objectivity, the Observer self gives us an edge. If we are able to watch things developing in our lives and if we are able to accept that some things are ending, we are free at the right moment to move into new areas and leave old areas behind.

This Rune also indicates that you have been making a lot of changes in yourself, your thoughts, your beliefs, in the recent past. A symbol of Perth is the soaring flight of the eagle. Indicating that you are learning to see far ahead and around you. Because of that, you are learning to make better decisions for your life.

Rune 2: Present

I drew Odin. Odin is the blank Rune. Some scholars dispute the use of Odin in Rune readings but I use it because it is the "zero" of the Runes. Think about how the lack of a zero would affect math. Odin fills in many spaces where we may forget to look if we aren't reminded about the unlimited potential of each present moment. You can see from that, how powerful Odin is in your spread. It reminds you of the unlimited potential of the present and it is in the Present position.

Like Perth, Odin also is concerned with things that are in the process of forming, which again strengthens its position and importance in your present life. Odin reminds us that there is a blank space as things in our lives form and there is a blank space as new things in our lives begin. You are being asked to trust the overall Universal Process in everyday life. Odin asks you to relinquish control of aspects of your life that have held you back and that you no longer need. What is asked at this point is for you to take time to think through what you would like to change about your life with objectivity and lack of judgment, and begin to make those changes. This Rune reminds you that the Universe is on your side. It can be scary or disruptive to make life changes, but they are necessary for growth.

Odin also reminds you that no matter what anyone else tries to hold you to, the past is the past. Karma is remade every day. Looking at life mathematically is helpful here. For example, a person who is made a scapegoat may in actuality be the sanest person in the group, because that person tries so hard to please the group. While the action/belief that pleasing the group is of paramount importance needs to change, the overall thread of the person's life would be one of service. That cancels out any of the other added on interpretations and beliefs from others.

What these first 2 Runes mean regarding your psychic sensitivities is that: Perth shows that you have been more and more aware of your gifts and Odin asks you to see them as good things and trust that the path that they are leading you along will be helpful for you.

Rune 3: Future

I drew Mannez, Rune of the Self. Mannez has to do with your identity as male or female and as a human being. Specifically, Mannez in the Future position is indicating that your psychic gifts will continue to show themselves and to develop as you allow them, and will change how you feel about your place in humanity. Mannez reminds us that our main focus in the development of our Self. It, too, is concerned with beginnings and endings. Why? Because each of us faces times in our lives when people believe things about us that are not true. To move past those wrong beliefs, we must change our beliefs about ourselves and risk showing our authentic self to the world.

Mannez is also a Rune of boundaries. It is up to each individual to define his or herself. We get to say, "No, what you said is not right about me," or "yes, that is true."

Mannez is again reminding you to use your Observer self. Watch what goes on but don't get involved unless it is in your best interest to do so. Above all, don't judge yourself or others. Simply note what is going on, and evaluate it. Mannez also indicates that the development of your psychic gifts is a natural part of your path and not something to be afraid of or worry about.

Rune 4: Underlying Energy (the force that is pushing this pattern forward).

I drew Gebo, Rune of Partnership.

Gebo reminds you that for any partnership to be healthy and happy, all members (or both, if it is a love partnership) must be equally respected. That's why Gebo looks like a capital "X." You can see that Gebo also appeared in your Future Rune, Mannez, which underlines the importance in your life now for equality, balance within yourself, trust among all members of yourself, (which also goes back to Odin) and inner and outer balance in your life. This Rune is asking you to consider all the aspects of your life and be willing to let any relationships go that are uneven.

Gebo also indicates the challenge to unite you with your Higher Self. The psychic gifts are an indication of your

Higher Self. You are being asked to trust that they are good things and that they will enhance your life.

Rune 5: A Possible Challenge

I drew Wunjo, Rune of Joy. Wunjo came up sideways, which is called Merkstave. This isn't a complete lack or reversal of joy, but an indication of the difficulty of the challenge you may have feeling joyous about your psychic gifts. Interestingly enough, your Future Rune, Mannez, is formed by making 2 Wunjo shapes facing each other, indicating that you will find joy, but that this is the challenge before you now.

Wunjo indicates that major battles in your life have been won. That it is Merkstave in your spread means that you will need to think carefully about what needs to change, think through what you will say and how you will handle the changes and then act. The Merkstave position also indicates that you are coming to yourself in some regard, possibly accepting your psychic gifts as natural abilities rather than something strange. The Rune scholars say that "the shift that was due has occurred." This Rune being on its side, though, indicates a bit of a struggle with that shift, which is why there are so many Runes beneath it that indicate the need for objectivity, acceptance, relinquishing of control and lack of judgment. Again, the presence of Mannez in the future indicates that you will make this shift.

A benefit of Wunjo is that the more you feel happy with yourself, the more others will feel happy around you. This will change your interaction with others.

Rune 6: A Possible Outcome

I drew Raido. This is the Rune of Communication. Since it looks like a capital "R", Raido, like Mannez, contains an element of joy, as in Wunjo. This indicates the need for extra reassurance that you will indeed find joy.

When you face challenges, remember that joy is promised three times in this spread. How you find it is to look for joy. Let other emotional energy threads pass by, and look for joy. You will find it.

Raido in the Outcome position is an excellent indicator that you will develop deeper inner communication, that you will learn to communicate through your psychic gifts, and that you will find balance. One of the meanings of Raido is the balance of issues that have more than one side. If you utilize the vantage point of the Objective self, you will be able to see many angles of life and that will allow you to move through life more freely. A main belief to consider changing is the belief that you need permission to exist and to be human.

Raido can also indicate opportunities to travel or to move into a new home, but also is concerned with your journey of self-healing. The more united you are as a person, the easier life will flow for you.

Rune 7: Confirmation

I drew Fehu. Fehu indicates a major success. This Rune is associated with monetary success but also can mean success in any area of our lives. Fehu in the Confirmation position in this spread is an indication that you will indeed find joy, and in finding that joy, many good things will come to you. This spread overall indicates that a lot of change is happening in your life. The more clearly you are able to see it and take advantage of it, the better off you will be.

Fehu asks you to think through what your beliefs about profit and gain are. In other words, what will make you happiest? Lots of money? Good friendships? What is most valuable to you, right now, in your life? Then just as you looked for the thread of joy, look for that thread in everything that happens in and around you every day. Fehu also asks you to value what you have learned.

You are in a time of change and some old beliefs may need to be released but that doesn't mean that what you learned in the past isn't valuable. Remember the lessons you've learned, the wisdom that you've gained. Perhaps keep a diary of all the psychic things that happen. When lights turn off, when you know a phone call is coming. Gather your evidence and keep it to help you believe that your gifts are real, true and valid. And valuable.

Remember to share any good fortune you have. Since this spread is focused on your psychic gifts, this indicates that you will benefit and grow if you are willing to share your gifts. Choose a divination tool and learn to use it. If Tarot feels too spooky, perhaps try Runes, since they are based on overall life themes, not on any specific group's philosophy.

Rising Spirals Rune Cast

The Rising Spirals Rune spread is a little like the Hidden Influences spread in the Tarot. The Rising Spirals Rune spread shows the path of your highest aspirations and intentions, paying special attention to any shadow energies that are difficult to see. It consists of five Runes, laid out in a spiraling pattern, bottom to top.

Rune 1: Origin of the Path

This Rune shows the beginning point of the life pattern under consideration. Like the source of a spring, this position can give insight into how the seeker has arrived at her present position. Knowing the source of a pattern also gives an opportunity to consider the choices that were made and how those choices have played out.

Rune 2: Development

This Rune shows how the initial idea or choice caused

the need for more choices and how the overall energetic thread developed over time. It may not have been clear at the time whether the choices that were made were the most helpful or not, but looking over the situation through the perspective of the Runes can give a different viewpoint, allowing for a more objective consideration of the situation.

Rune 3: Aspirations

Rune three shows how the energies associated with Runes 1 and 2 played out as far as overall life goals are concerned. If, for example, the source of the energy pattern under consideration was feeling stuck, then the development in Rune 2 may have been to create some kind of movement, make some decision. Rune 3 begins to show whether the decision made at Rune 2 helped or hindered the original situation.

Rune 4: Feedback

This Rune shows how others responded to the changes and decisions that were made. For example, if a person were to choose to take up a new hobby, some friends would probably welcome the new interest, while others might be miffed. As in Rune 3, the goal is to develop an objective stance. Use this Rune position to simply look at how others responded to the choices that were made. Remember that the choices were neither perfect nor wrong, and that no matter what changes we make in our lives, some people will approve, while others will not.

Nevertheless, feedback is a helpful tool for gaining perspective.

Rune 5: Hopes and Dreams

Rune 5 gives perspective into how well the chosen path is working in the seeker's life thus far. It's interesting to note that Rune 5 can be seen in a similar way as an outcome, or can be the beginning of a new spiral. If, after considering the pattern, the seeker chooses to begin a new path by selecting different choices, the seeker may return to the original source point and begin a new pattern, or take a different direction.

The seeker can also work from the Hopes and Dreams point, extrapolating from the energy pattern indicated by Rune 5, either to modify the current path or enhance it.

Here is a sample Rising Spirals Rune Cast:

Rune 1: Origin of the Path
• Wunjo, Rune of Joy

Drawing Wunjo in the Origin position indicates a foundation of joy is the basis of your life. Though the Rune that appears in the development position will give more insight into how you are manifesting and expressing joy in your life, having Wunjo as the Origin of your current life path gives a positive energetic tone to your life at this time.

Rune 2: Development of the Path
• Ehwaz, Rune of Steady Forward Motion.

Ehwaz is concerned with consistent, steady growth, forward motion; unstoppable motion such as the movement of the sun across the sky. This indicates that the path you created, with one of the expected outcomes being a happy or joyful one, has a solid foundation. There is an aspect in the combination of Ehwaz and Wunjo that can indicate the need for cautious expression of joy rather than total openness of your inner motives but the sun peeks through all aspects of your life and your current project or path as surely as it moves across the sky each day. Even when the light of the sun is covered by clouds, it's still there.

Rune 3: Aspirations

- Mannez, The Source Rune, Reversed.

Drawing Mannez in the Aspirations position indicates that your main focus for choosing the path you are currently on is that of improving your sense of self, which is the core focus of Rune lore. As you become more balanced within yourself, you will be more comfortable with other people and others will be drawn to you because of your calm and joyful nature.

Another aspect of Mannez in the Aspirations position is that you have chosen this energetic path in order to continue to challenge and balance yourself and come into harmony with your inner and outer selves.

Rune 4: Feedback

- Ansuz, Rune of the Divine: The Writer's Rune

Drawing Ansuz in the Feedback position indicates communication is flowing to you and from you simultaneously. One reason Ansuz is the Rune of the Divine is its connection to the god Loki. Loki has a tendency to turn events that could be seen as challenges or even disasters into opportunities instead.

Loki shifts the emphasis of our life challenges by whispering the secrets of the Gods into our ears. This is one reason that Ansuz is also called the Writer's Rune. If we take the opportunity to listen carefully to the whispered voice, we can come up with ideas, inspirations, words, understanding and wisdom that others don't know.

In this way we can see Ansuz as a writer's or artist's muse. In this particular Rune cast, Ansuz is strengthening the path that was created in joy, developed at a steady pace and from the perspective of developing the inner and outer sense of self.

Rune 5: Hopes and Dreams

- Algiz, Rune of Protection.

Drawing the Rune of Protection in the Hopes and Dreams position of the Rising Spirals Rune Cast indicates that your current project, concern or path is protected. I hope you can see that overall, this Rune cast indicates a strong, well thought out path that is still developing. Drawing Algiz in the final position indicates that you will be able to continue to move along this path, and that your interests will be protected.

More Insight on the Developing Path

If you would like more insight into the development of the current path, wait a week or so, then deliberately draw the final Rune from the previous cast (which is one reason that it's a good idea to note the Runes drawn in each cast).

In this case, you would draw Ansuz and ask the Rune for any wisdom it can add since the last time it was cast. Jot down any insights that come to you, then return Ansuz to the Rune bag and draw the Rising Spirals Rune Cast again.

In this case, Ansuz can come up again, but it is also a foundational energy that informs the overall energy of the current Rune cast. You can repeat this Rune cast weekly, each time using the last Rune drawn in the previous cast, to continue to shed light on your current project.

Once your project is complete, and the energies tied to the Runes will show you when that is, take a moment to thank the Runes for their guidance and spend time carefully planning a new path.

Runes that indicate that a path is complete: Thurisaz, Dagaz, Perth, Odin.

Chapter 14:
Runic Energetic Interpretations

My definitions of the Runes follow the energetic threads of the messages contained in each Rune. These interpretations come from a combination of intuiting with the Runes themselves as well as studying the writings of Ralph H. Blum, Nigel Pennic, Donald Tyson, Tony Willis and others, the emphasis being on my intuition with the Runes themselves.

I have included the element (earth, air, water, fire, metal) associated with each Rune as well as the Chakra, deity, polarity, color, Universal message and associated emotions.

Fehu: Rune of the Rising Spiral

Fehu energy is concerned with the physical, emotional, energetic and spiritual things that are most important to you. That can include how important possessions are to you, what role they play in your life, how accessible you believe abundance is and how deeply you value qualities such as compassion, generosity and integrity.

Fehu asks you to be concerned not just how you will care for yourself but with what it means to you to be cared for. This energy challenges you to think carefully about how much you value yourself.

Though Fehu's energy can indicate physical as well as energetic blessings, remember that even unexpected blessings aren't free. The "fee" attached to Fehu's blessings is an increased awareness and the challenge to use abundance wisely. In fact, the "fee" in Fehu's name is the origin of our meaning "fee" or payment.

One of Fehu's ancient ties was to livestock like cattle and sheep. This represented not only wealth and possessions, since livestock create more livestock and therefore can create wealth, but also the movability of wealth. Many people have won millions of dollars in the lottery, for example, only to return to their original state of non-abundance after a short time. Wealth can rise and fall, but our sense of our inner worth is a permanent source of riches.

The more flexible you are with your ability to plan, the more likely you are to succeed because that flexibility gives you a broader perspective. Fehu also encourages you to share what you have with others. This is not just speaking of sharing physical wealth, but sharing emotional wealth such as wisdom, psychic lessons and energies and life lessons as well.

Fehu's ultimate message is to remind you that the biggest rewards come from the Universe, the place of unlimited resources. If your goal in life is to value the time, relationships and the energy you have been given, the rewards you receive will be more than you could ever have imagined.

Fehu also counsels you to value the lessons you have been taught. It's easy to be careful when you're on a tight budget, but Fehu asks you to remember the principles you have learned when you have plenty.

Fehu challenges you to think carefully about how you use money and credit. Though it offers you the power to gain worldly wealth and the focused intent necessary to keep it, remember that the main area of control is the control of the self.

Even if Fehu brings you winnings, windfalls, luck, abundance and/or financial strength, remember that wealth brings responsibilities. Success can give you "wings" of a sort, by providing the energy and foresight to move freely in the world.

Element: Air

Polarity: Rune of Balance

Color: Light Red, indicating the need to work on the stabilizing of the Root Chakra. Since the Root Chakra is concerned with the lower back, sciatica, varicose veins, rectal bleeding, depression, immune disorders and osteoarthritis, if the Seeker has any of these physical ailments, the wisdom of this Rune can speak to those issues as well as emotional or spiritual issues.

Deity: Freyja. Freyja is a goddess associated with love, beauty, fertility and gold (wealth), but also with war and death. Freyja is said to rule the afterlife, giving the impression that if we have not dealt fairly with people in our present life, Freyja may be waiting with her sword to mete out justice in the afterlife. Odin may plead for mercy on our behalf but it is Freyja who will decide what will happen.

Universal Law: Our worth comes from the Universe, not from any other source. The wealth of inner wisdom and psychic messages are more lasting and therefore more valuable than physical wealth.

Reversed: Frustration. Observe the pattern of frustration and falling short, asking, "What do I need to learn from this?" Recognize where your true nourishment comes from. Whenever you have a need, go to the Universe for help instead of relying completely on people or other physical sources.

Emotions: Inner worth, attitude about gain or loss of property, self-esteem, when upright. Failure, greed, burnout, atrophy, cowardice, stupidity, dullness, poverty, slavery, bondage when Reversed.

Uruz: Rune of Empowerment

Uruz is concerned with inner and outer strength, as well as the idea that not all types of strength can be controlled, manipulated or domesticated. The latter is one reason that the Rune Uruz is connected to the wild ox, which cooperated to a certain extent with its human owners but never became completely tame. A modern-day example would be an elephant that works with people but doesn't give its complete loyalty to anyone but its herd.

Uruz gives strength to begin new projects and to draw the line when the time comes to end a project, relationship, partnership or friendship. Uruz reminds you that nothing in this life is permanent by calling to mind the natural patterns of life: Death, Decay, Fertilization, Gestation and Rebirth.

As such, Uruz is the Rune of passage, reminding you that all aspects of life have their time and place. Endings and beginnings are only as painful as you make them. The more quickly you can accept the things that come and go in your life and get on with your life's purpose, the easier the life cycles will be.

Despite its focus on having the strength to make what may be at times unpopular or difficult decisions, the main energy behind Uruz is that of positive growth and change. If a relationship is holding you back, for example, Uruz can give you the strength to navigate the choppy waters of transition so that you can find smoother sailing ahead. Seeing even the difficult aspects of growth as a choice is empowering and strengthening.

The perspective of Uruz is that the new life you are creating is always greater than the old. Once you have made the necessary changes, your life will change for the better and your inner and outer sense of self will become stronger.

Element: Earth.

Polarity: Male

Color: Dark green, indicating the need to work on the Heart Chakra. Since the Heart Chakra is concerned with heart conditions, asthma, lung and breast cancers, middle (thoracic) spine, pneumonia, upper back, shoulders and high blood pressure, if the Seeker has any of these physical issues, the wisdom of Uruz can speak to those issues as well as emotional or spiritual issues.

Deity: Urdl, also called Ullr in the Old Norse. Urdl is associated with glory. Little is known of Urdl except for the reference to glory, but if you look at the energy of the Rune Uruz linked with the energy of glory, you can see that to wield the energy you have been given in ways that engender peace, prosperity and balance is a glorious thing, indeed.

Universal Message: The Universe gives each of us our own unique strength. Learning to wield it correctly is part of the life path. Even when change is difficult, having the strength and courage to trust the Universe above and beyond human relationships or understanding is always to your advantage.

Reversed: You may miss opportunities or advantages if you don't listen carefully to the wisdom of your heart, or if you try to manipulate situations to make them go your way.

Using brute strength can deplete your available life energy as well as push others away, reducing your available sources and resources.

Your own strength could be used against you if you push too hard. Depending on how aware, or unaware, you are, minor or major failures and disappointments can occur. Uruz reversed counsels you to set the highest priority as the quality of your relationship to yourself.

Emotions: Use of strength, understanding of empowerment, your perception of the meaning and purpose of strength when Upright. Weakness, obsession, misdirected force, domination by others, sickness, inconsistency, ignorance, lust, brutality, violence when Reversed.

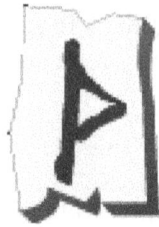

Thurisaz: Rune of the Energetic Gateway

Thurisaz is sometimes seen as a thorn that can prick you, to goad you into moving in a new direction or to nudge you past a reluctance to enter a new area or field of thoughts. This Rune is a gateway—a place of careful consideration.

The energy behind Thurisaz' thorn reminds you that the thing you push against lifts you up. Yes, there is a risk of being pricked but if you don't try, you won't rise. If you carefully move the thorny branches aside, or use the thorns to climb, you may pass through the area safely.

Passing through the difficult channels of life requires creative energy if you are to get through unscathed. Once you have passed beyond the thorns, the prickly barrier can serve as a defense or attack against adversaries.

Thurisaz also offers deep, penetrating wisdom, since those who know how to get out of a tight spot show a high degree of wisdom. This effect is strengthened when this Rune is combined with Sowelu, the Rune of Wholeness. When combined with Nauthis, Rune of Self-Reliance, Thurisaz becomes a regenerative catalyst, urging you past obstacles into new areas.

In short, Thurisaz offers the opportunity to leave behind the patterns and habits that are no longer serving you and brings you to a place where you have the perspective to think though your past before moving into the future.

Thurisaz challenges you to move with both yin and yang energy, as it takes inner and outer work to prepare to enter a new space. Only when the inner work of consulting our Higher Self and contacting the Divine has been completed are you prepared to begin a new outer work.

And so, you are asked to approach Thurisaz' gateway with respect and contemplation. If you are willing to do this, Thurisaz will send you a clear reflection of your life's journey up to this point. Consider what you are shown then bless all of your past, the triumphs and the mistakes, without judgment. Thurisaz is not the place of judgment, only of consideration. Once you have gained the perspective of thinking through your life, release it.

This is how you reclaim your power. This is when you are ready to step through the gate.

Element: Fire

Color: Red, indicating attention is needed for the Root Chakra. Since the Root Chakra is concerned with the lower back, sciatica, varicose veins, rectal bleeding, depression, immune disorders and osteoarthritis, if the Seeker has any of these physical ailments, the wisdom of this Rune can speak to those issues as well as emotional or spiritual issues.

Polarity: Rune of Balance

Deity: Thor. Thor is one of the thunder gods in Norse mythology. Thor is sometimes called the father of Odin and sometimes Thor is the son of Odin, which makes sense in a way, since Odin is called both the beginning and the end. Two of Thor's most memorable attributes were his famous hammer, that he named Mjolnir and his belt of strength named Megingjardir. Thor reminds you that the core of your strength lies in your ability to deeply integrate and accept life's lessons and challenges.

Universal Law: Whenever your life path shifts and you prepare to enter a new energetic space or channel, take a few moments to look over the path you have traveled. Realize that this is a holy moment. Thank the energies, spirits and helpers who have brought you this far. Then take a deep breath, look to the future and leave behind the things you no longer need. Then, with reverence, step through the new gateway.

Reversed: Life circumstances are pushing you toward change and growth. Even if you feel pressed, take time out to express your gratitude for the distance from which you have traveled, to integrate the messages and lessons of your life's path. If you find yourself resenting the feeling of being pushed, remember that stressful times are part of life. What we call "suffering" is just the experiences of what we need to grow.

It's important not to be hasty or leap ahead too far. One reason to consider where you have been is so you can see more clearly where you are. If there is any doubt about the direction, a wise choice is to wait on the will of the Universe.

Emotions: Challenge, encouragement, perspective and perseverance when Upright. Danger, defenselessness, compulsion, betrayal, dullness, malice, hatred, torment, spite, rape when Reversed.

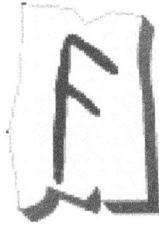

Ansuz: Rune of the Divine Muse/Writer's Rune

Ansuz is concerned with signals received and signals given. It is a messenger Rune, so you are wise to consider information from unusual sources when Ansuz is drawn. The messages Ansuz is concerned with are usually from Divine sources, Spirit Guides, animal guides and/or concerning Divine sources such as elementals, Spirit Guides, Gods and Goddesses. Ansuz is an expression of the Divine breath that powers all of existence.

Another aspect of Ansuz is that it is concerned with energetic messages, such as the sudden flash of inspiration that transforms a project or helps to form a story, book or play, which is why I also call it the Writer's Rune.

The emphasis of the wisdom offered by Ansuz is in hearing and listening, in preparation for teaching. Since the ultimate concern of the Runes is the development of the self, Ansuz also directs you to consider the Divine Source within yourself and all human beings. The Divine may seem as if it is out of your reach. Ansuz reminds you that the Divine is always near.

Ansuz is also the energetic indicator of consciousness and intellectual activities. If you carefully consider both inner and outer wisdom and if you have the courage to rely on your inner guidance, even when outer sources don't agree, blessings, support and help will come from unexpected sources. This is because Ansuz helps you to integrate unconscious motive with conscious intent, which is also a form of self-nourishment.

Ansuz reminds you that the Divine order stands firm no matter how difficult life is. This means that no matter how much outer chaos or drama exists, Divine stability will eventually win out. This Rune can indicate that by relying on inner wisdom, a new or deeper sense of familial unity can be achieved. Perhaps an estrangement can be mended or a misunderstanding cleared up.

Ansuz doesn't always give you the answers you want to hear but it does offer revealing messages or insight. Part of the answer may be in naming of things that have been blocked or hidden in the past. Ansuz reminds you that there is power in words, so you are advised to choose your words wisely.

Element: Air

Polarity: Rune of balance.

Color: Dark blue, indicating a need to consider the Throat Chakra. Since the Throat Chakra is connected with sore throat, mouth ulcers, scoliosis, swollen glands, thyroid dysfunctions, tonsillitis, laryngitis, voice problems and gum or tooth issues, the wisdom of the Rune can speak to those issues as well as emotional or spiritual issues.

Ansuz is also connected to the Third Eye Chakra. Since the Third Eye Chakra is concerned with brain tumors, strokes, blindness, deafness, seizures and learning disabilities, this Rune can speak to these issues as well as emotional and spiritual issues.

Deity: The Norse God Loki. Loki is the ancient trickster of the Norse gods as well as a bringer of benefits to humankind. Loki stole fire from Thor's forge to give mankind the benefit of that element. Loki indicates that even if some people disagree with you or are trying to thwart your plans, that unusual and often unseen help is still on your side. Loki also reminds you that even thieves and scoundrels can be the bearers of wisdom. It's all a matter of perspective. Loki himself was viewed as a thief by the other gods and as a hero by humanity.

Universal Message: The angels, Spirit Guides, and the Source Itself are always available to you, to offer support, guidance, validation and advice. All you need to do is listen.

Reverse: When reversed, Ansuz is concerned with failed communication; specifically, with the failure to listen. Failure to listen or insistence on teaching when you are still a student can result in a lack of clarity or awareness. Drawing Ansuz Reversed challenges you to consider areas where you are in denial or are refusing to listen. Denial can be an indication of yin deficiency since yin is concerned with allowing the self to be nurtured, cherished, appreciated or taught.

To right this imbalance, the Universe sends of opportunities to be taught or nurtured. The more willing you are to receive what is offered, the easier the process will go. This is one of the Runes where patience is its own reward.

Ansuz also reminds you that what is happening is necessary for your personal growth. This Rune also asks you to become more flexible. If it seems as if everyone around you is saying "no", think about the themes that are presenting themselves to find out why. Remember that life is like a game in some ways. Once you know the lessons contained in a particular energetic thread, you won't need to visit the uncomfortable places so often.

Emotions: Hearing, listening, muse, deciphering, when Upright. Misunderstanding, delusion, manipulation by others, boredom, vanity, impatience when Reversed.

Raido: Rune of the Soul's Journey

Raido is the Rune of the soul's journey because its main focus is on communication and developing the patience and expertise to bring about union or reunion, especially in life areas where there are two sides that need to come into harmony.

Raido reminds you that the Ultimate Union is when what is above and what is below are of one mind and working in harmony. In a way, the above and below aspect is the ultimate example of two sides that need to come into harmony.

The balancing aspect of Raido also speaks to the idea of inner worth. How do you feel about yourself, deep down? Do you welcome and accept yourself as an aspect of the universe or do you consider yourself to be a lesser being or even separate from the rest of creation?

Whatever the case, you will grow closer to the Ultimate Union if you consider your sense of self, actions and words through prayer, meditation or soul seeking.

If life doesn't make sense or if you feel you need more time, Raido challenges you to value yourself enough to take it. If others don't seem to understand you, don't worry. Raido reminds you that a soul's journey must be traveled alone.

The cyclic nature of the lessons learned in each life reminds you of the motion of a wheel, since life is the vehicle you use to learn and grow and develop the soul. The cyclic nature of Raido also underlines the importance of rites and ceremonies, which can help to focus or channel your energies in effective ways.

Raido also reminds you that the experiences of each life provide the transformation for your spirit self to move from one place to another. Raido energy can indicate a physical move to a new home or living space, so drawing it when you are considering a move is a sign of support from the Universe. This Rune can also indicate a need to shift your point of view.

An aspect that is rarely considered when Raido is drawn is its connection to music. The word "Raid" is the Norse word for music. Vibration is an important aspect of all types of transformation, movement, change and growth, so consider the uses of music in your life when Raido is drawn. Raido might be asking you to think about your personal rhythm and the world rhythm around you. Or, more specifically, how your personal rhythm harmonizes, or doesn't, with the bigger rhythms around you.

Raido energy indicates the need for dedicated practice and planning to bring out balance. Drawing this Rune in combination with Dagaz indicates that you are in the right place at the right time.

Elements: Air/Water

Color: Bright red, indicating the need for grounding in general, and for consideration of and clearing, balancing and filling the Root Chakra. Since the Root Chakra is concerned with the lower back, sciatica, varicose veins, rectal bleeding, depression, immune disorders and osteoarthritis, if the Seeker has any of these physical ailments, the wisdom of this Rune can speak to those issues as well as emotional or spiritual issues.

Polarity: Rune of Balance

Deities: Ing. Ing is a God of fertility, of home and family life, as well as a protector of the family and house. Ing also insured good catches of fish and game, as well as bountiful harvests. Ing also represented the healthy and productive side of sexuality, bringing up yet another life thread where two sides can come into alignment.

Nerthus: A mysterious Danish goddess who is sometimes also known as Hertha. She is usually portrayed nude and amply endowed, which speaks to the sexual aspects of balancing and harmonizing from the perspective of two sides. Nerthus is also known as an ancient Germanic goddess who Tacitus refers to as Mother Earth, claiming that she was worshiped at a temple in a sacred grove on an island in the Baltic Sea. Whenever her presence was among her people, they lived in peace.

Universal Law: Inner balance is essential when you need to make life changes, especially big changes like changing jobs or moving to a new home, or changes that affect others. Also, when you live in balance and harmony, you will live in peace.

Reversed: Be attentive to personal relationships, ruptured relationships. How you respond is up to you. Detours, inconveniences, disruptions are actually opportunities to take a new direction.

Emotions: Balance, harmony, expertise, clarity of intent and focus when Upright. Crisis, rigidity, stasis, injustice, irrationality, disruption, especially when combined with Hagalaz, dislocation, demotion, delusion, losing one's way, possible death when Reversed.

Kano: Rune of Transforming Knowledge

Kano is the Rune of opening; specifically the kind of opening that creates insight and understanding that transforms your current life path. Kano is the Rune that lights that way, so is associated with a torch or fire. Just as turning on a light or lighting a fire reveals things hidden in the dark, so the energy of Kano provides a clearer focus and allows for greater clarity in your life. A Rune of beginnings, Kano frees you to see clearly enough to remove inner and outer clutter so that you are ready to receive new gifts, which opens the door to a deeper joy of life.

Kano's clarity also speaks of mutual respect and openness in relationships.

Kano's "aha!" moments help you to absorb lessons and guide your own students with directness and balance. Kano's ability to see to the heart of a matter gives power to all positive actions. This is the power of the transforming forge that molds the mortal into something new.

Kano's energy can also cause discomfort, especially if its light hits an area of your life that you aren't ready to look at. Just as bright light can cause your eyes to tear, Kano's revealing light can challenge you to look into areas of your life that need attention.

Kano's energy is also concerned with creativity, inspiration and technical ability, urging you to hone your skills and to surrender to the Forge of the Universe itself. The power of Kano is the harnessed power of fire: the warming, enlightening energy that transforms a frigid winter's night into a snug place of contemplation.

Combined with Raido, Kano is the energy of regeneration, reminding you that seeing a bigger perspective gives you more flexibility to create your own reality.

Element: Fire

Color: Light red, indicating the need to balance the energies of the Root and/or Sacral Chakra. Since the Root Chakra is concerned with the lower back, sciatica, varicose veins, rectal bleeding, depression, immune disorders and osteoarthritis, if the Seeker has any of these physical ailments, and the Sacral Chakra is concerned with ob/gyn problems, pelvic pain and urinary issues, the wisdom of this Rune can speak to those issues as well as emotional or spiritual issues.

Polarity: Rune of Balance

Deities: Heimdall. Heimdall is the god of the resounding horn. Heimdall's energy is that of charging forward, riding his golden-maned horse, Gulltoppr. His appearance can be sudden and his light startling. He has a strong sense of foreknowledge and sharp hearing and eyesight. His motives are so pure that he is known as "the whitest of the gods".[20]

Freyja: Freyja is a goddess associated with love, beauty, fertility, gold, but also war and death. Freyja is said to rule the afterlife, giving the impression that if you have not dealt fairly with people in your present life, Freyja may be waiting with her sword to mete out justice in the afterlife. Odin may

---

[20] http://en.wikipedia.org/Heimdall

plead for mercy on your behalf but it is Freyja who will decide what will happen.

Universal Law: Inspiration. Nothing can remain hidden or dark forever. Diligent seeking will always gain results and provide insight, challenge and inspiration.

Reversed: Darkening of a situation, closing of a relationship. Closing of a mind, an opinion, ending of a friendship. Kano reversed asks you to develop inner stability, give up old ways, and live empty for awhile.

Emotions: Clarity, illumination, openness when Upright. Disease, breakup, instability, lack of creativity, nakedness, exposure, loss of illusion, false hope when Reversed.

Gebo: Rune of Energetic Exchange

Gebo is concerned with the energetic thread of partnerships of all kinds, including business, marital and friendships. Gebo reminds you that a true partnership is a gift, because true partnerships require all parties to be equal and balanced.

Since the main goal of Rune readings is the development of the self, seeing the self as a gift to others is an important aspect. Partnerships that are based on equality and mutual respect give the ultimate gift: the freedom for all concerned to be true to the partnership without sacrificing their sense of self.

Another aspect of Gebo is exchanges of energy of all kinds. These can include small talk in the grocery line, gifts, and business contacts. If Gebo shows up in your life today, a windfall may be coming your way. The manner of gifts offered by Gebo is different from Fehu in that the gift or gifts might be small rather than large, will be something unexpected or will come in an unexpected way. This can also indicate that a talent or skill that you have been developing will begin to produce or you will have an opportunity to develop a talent or skill.

Since Gebo is Rune number seven in the Elder Futhark, this is where the idea of "lucky seven" has come from.

Since your own personal presence is necessary to form the ultimate partnership, Gebo is also concerned with health issues. Remember that you have the right at any time to reconsider, slow down, or even stop the process. If allow yourself to be pushed farther than it is safe for you to go, your health may call attention to itself in order to slow you down.

Gebo reminds you that you can reconsider any agreement, even agreements you make with yourself. If you deny one part of yourself in order to express another part, the part that is repressed can cause health challenges, so Gebo also urges you to keep yourself as balanced as possible.

Remember that the ultimate partnership is not between us and other people, but is the ultimate link or union with the Higher Self and the Universe. This creates unity between the giver and the receiver in any circumstance.

Gebo's ultimate gift is to help you to recognize the Divine aspects in all things—including you! Yes, that means rocks, trees and water but it also means seeing the Divine even in the most mundane circumstances. This perspective can transform everyday or frustrating circumstances into adventures of wonder and validation.

Gebo's "X" shape indicates balance & harmony. Living in balance and harmony creates an atmosphere in which unexpected and/or unasked for gifts may be received or exchanged. Gebo can also speak to unions such as marriage.

Gebo's greatest gift is to illuminate the path that leads to inner balance.

Element: Air/polarity

Color: Dark blue. Corresponds to the Throat Chakra. Speaking your truth and being heard, offering a service or being offered a service or favor, and returning the service or favor. Since the Throat Chakra is connected with sore throat, mouth ulcers, scoliosis, swollen glands, thyroid dysfunctions, tonsillitis, laryngitis, voice problems and gum or tooth issues, the wisdom of the Rune can speak to those issues as well as emotional or spiritual issues.

Gebo is also connected to the Third Eye Chakra. Since the Third Eye Chakra is concerned with brain tumors, strokes, blindness, deafness, seizures and learning disabilities, this Rune can speak to these issues as well as emotional and spiritual issues

Polarity: Rune of Balance

Deities: Odin. Odin is one of the primary Norse gods, considered by some sources to be a shape shifter.[21] Odin is considered to be a leader of souls, though the direction he chooses to lead may not be as clear as you may prefer. Odin is often depicted on horseback, holding a spear in one hand and accompanied by a raven.

Gefn: The Norse Goddess Gefn is one of the lesser-known names for Freyja. Freyja is a goddess associated with love, beauty, fertility, gold, but also war and death. Freyja is said to rule the afterlife, giving the impression that if we have not dealt fairly with people in our present life, Freyja may be waiting with her sword to mete out justice in the afterlife. Odin may plead for mercy on our behalf but it is Freyja who will decide what will happen.

Universal Message: You are worthy of being treated fairly and of treating yourself fairly.

Gebo has no reverse, but if Gebo is Merkstave this can indicate opposition, greed loneliness, dependence, divorce, sacrifice, obligation.

---

[21] http://en.wikipedia.org/wiki/Odin

Emotions: Love, respect, mutuality, giving, compassion, fairness, balance when Upright. Opposition, greed, loneliness, dependence divorce when Merkstave.

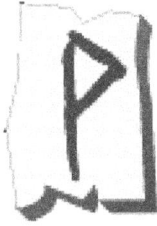

Wunjo: Rune of Joy and Fellowship

Wunjo is the Rune of joy and light. If Wunjo has shown up in your life today, this is an indication that you are allowing the energy of joy to flow through your life, which is allowing you to be more successful. Joy will not flow if there is inner struggle so if Wunjo appears in a Rune cast, this indicates that you have come to know and appreciate yourself through times of difficulty and struggle.

Your body/mind/spirit has been honed and prepared to receive spiritual and physical blessings. Energy and clarity that has been blocked in the past is able to flow through you freely now. The flowing of Wunjo's waters through your self creates the freshness of restoration.

The whirlpools and rapids of feeling lonely and of anxiety have disappeared. Wunjo is a Rune of fellowship and well-being. As we realize our true nature and path, we are able to spread joy with our presence to all we meet.

Wunjo's good news can come in many forms, as good news from afar, as comfort, pleasure; as fellowship or friendship when combined with Gebo and as prosperity, especially when combined with Fehu.

Element: Wind

Color: Light blue, indicating the need to stabilize the energy of the Throat Chakra. Since the Throat Chakra is connected with sore throat, mouth ulcers, scoliosis, swollen glands, thyroid dysfunctions, tonsillitis, laryngitis, voice problems and gum or tooth issues, the wisdom of the Rune can speak to those issues as well as emotional or spiritual issues.

Polarity: Female

Deities: Odin. Odin is one of the primary Norse gods, considered by some sources to be a shape shifter. Odin is considered to be a leader of souls, though the direction he chooses to lead may not be as clear as we may prefer. Odin is often depicted on horseback, holding a spear in one hand and accompanied by a raven.

Frigg: Frigg, also known as Freyja or Frigga, is a major Norse goddess. She is said to be the wife of Odin, and is the "foremost among the goddesses" and the queen of Asgard. Frigg appears primarily in Norse mythological stories as a wife and a mother. She is also described as having the power of prophecy yet she does not reveal what she knows. Frigg is described as the only one other than Odin who is permitted to sit on his high seat Hlidskjalf and look out over the universe. The English term Friday derives from the Anglo-Saxon name for Frigg, Frige.

Universal Law: Compassion. Showing deep compassion for yourself helps you to become aligned with the harmonies of the Universe, which brings fellowship and great joy.

Reversed: Wunjo reversed may indicate a delay in your ability to receive joy or a blockage in your recognition of your true self. As you can imagine, an inability to accept joy or a lack of self-knowledge can create challenges that otherwise wouldn't need to be in your life.

A wise gardener once taught me that when a plant won't grow, go back to the basics and see where the chain of growth has been broken. You can do the same if you are blocking joy. Follow the thread of joy backward in your life until you reach the place where the difficulty in accepting or feeling deserving of joy began. Then, lay a new path, gradually accepting more and more joy into your life until your life is brimming over with inner happiness.

The acknowledgment of any refusal or blockage of joy in your life is a signal from the Universe, to help you. One way to begin accepting joy into your life is to focus on the present, on how you will benefit from learning the lesson put before you. Be sincere and trust yourself. Remember, all of life's lessons are designed to help you to develop and understand your deepest self. No matter what, you cannot fail.

Emotions: Joy, fulfillment, peace and compassion when Upright. Sorrow, alienation, delirium, intoxication, loss of sense of self, impractical enthusiasm, raging frenzy, berserker when Reversed.

Hagalaz: Rune of the Strong Will

The energy of the Rune Hagalaz is strong-willed and disruptive, very much like a sudden hailstorm in spring or summer or a single-minded person intent on getting her way. While it may be tempting to see this Rune as a negative energy, remember that sudden, strong shifts in energy can also free you to make changes, clarify intentions and explore new areas of life.

When you think of elemental energy such as a storm, you may think of things happening *to* you. But what if *you* are the storm? What if it is your decisions that are whipping up the waters around other people's boats, so to speak?

Many life changes affect others as strongly as they affect us. We may find a wild ride through the storm clouds of change to be exhilarating, but others may feel as if their foundation has shifted out from under them. This is part of the untamable aspect of Hagalaz energy.

If there are areas in your life where you have felt stuck, the energy of Hagalaz can bring a sense of inner awakening that gives you the strength you need to push through any snags. If a gentler change is needed, Hagalaz energy can enter your life in a more gradual way that leads you to gradual changes.

Hagalaz energy may announce itself in the sudden realization that a business deal, friendship, partnership or plan is failing. But even if what is fading out of your life is something important to you, don't give up. Hagalaz provides the dis-illusioning awakening for you to see that change is needed, as well as a burst of inner strength to guide you and provide insight into what you need to do next.

If you are receiving a cold shoulder from someone, or feeling compelled to freeze someone out of your life, remember that the energy of Hagalaz can be icy, especially if combined with Isa.

Hagalaz also speaks of the laws of existence by revealing to your conscious mind the pattern of events in your past that has shaped your present. This sudden moment of "aha!" can help you to see what areas need to be weeded out. Remember, too, that the melting ice after a hailstorm helps the garden to grow.

Combined with Nauthiz, Hagalaz can indicate cranky energy that leads to stagnation and loss of power, which causes physical and/or emotional pain. In this case, reground yourself, clarify your goals and reset your boundaries. When you reach a place of calm, move forward again.

Elements: Wind and Water

Color: Light blue, indicating a need to consider balancing, clearing and/or filling the Throat Chakra. Since the Throat Chakra is connected with sore throat, mouth ulcers, scoliosis, swollen glands, thyroid dysfunctions, toncillitus, laryngitis, voice problems and gum or tooth issues, the wisdom of the Rune can speak to those issues as well as emotional or spiritual issues.

Polarity: Rune of Balance

Deities: Urdl, also called Ullr in the Old Norse. Urdl is associated with glory. Little is known of Urdl except for the reference to glory, but as we look at the energy of the Rune Hagalz linked with the energy of glory, we can see that to make the changes we need in order to have a balanced life is a glorious thing, indeed.

Heimdall, which is also spelled Hiemdallr. This Norse god has a horn that he blasts to call attention to major events. He rides the golden-maned horse Gulltoppr, has gold teeth and is the son of the Nine Mothers. Heimdall's influence helps you to focus on relationships to resolve conflicts and face disappointment and defeat.

Universal Law: Whenever there is change, something is disrupted. Whether you create change that disrupts your normal pattern or the pattern of others, know that the upheaval is a necessary part of growth and healing.

Merkstave: Since Hagalaz has no reverse, it can also be read in a sideways, or Merkstave, position. Drawing Hagalaz in a Merkstave position still indicates a storm, but perhaps this will be a lesser storm. Perhaps you are at a level of awareness where you are able to see the decisions you need to make and set firm boundaries.

Hagalaz in the Merkstave position can also indicate an emotional storm that blusters and soon blows itself out. A key here is not to take the emotional energy personally. If you are able to observe it and let it pass, you can learn from the energy or perhaps even find gifts blown in by the storm itself.

If the Merkstave Hagalaz is speaking of your energy, it could indicate that your bark is worse than your bite—that you talk a lot but don't have the energy to follow through.

Emotions: Inner and outer energy, strong-willed, ability to create change when Upright. Emotional storm, catastrophe, loss, suffering, hardship, sickness, crisis, ineffectiveness when Merkstave.

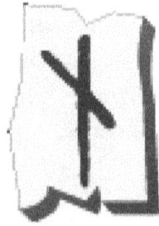

Nauthiz: Rune of Self-Reliance

Nauthiz is the Rune of self-reliance because it is often through situations when the people you count on let you down or when you feel that life itself has let you down that you learn to rely on yourself.

The uncomfortable feeling of constraint, brought out perhaps by lack of basic necessities such as clothing, housing, employment and transportation can urge you to find a way to a create more comfortable life for yourself. Perhaps you can learn a new skill or move to a different area. Even parting with unnecessary clutter can free up the energy around you.

Nauthiz energy is valuable because it helps you to identify your shadow or repressed side. A main lesson to learn from the energy of Nauthiz: Don't take life too personally or project your own inner weaknesses onto others. As long as you allow drama to run your life, Nauthiz will be your faithful friend, teaching you the importance of self-control.

What helps to break free from Nauthiz energy? Learn to laugh at yourself. Keep moving forward. If you offend someone, apologize or make it right. If you owe anyone anything—money, a favor, etc, take care of those issues. This way you will gradually restore harmony and balance in your life.

Another aspect of Nauthiz energy is that the things that make you feel uncomfortable can be seen as kindling to spark your inner fire of self-reliance. In ancient times, a

"Need Fire" was a powerful signal that was only lit in times of disasters like natural calamity or epidemic. Nauthiz energy is a lot like a "Need Fire", calling your attention to areas of your life where you are or could become stuck.

The power of Nauthiz is that it transforms the power to be released from needs—the uncomfortable constriction or pain of habits. When combined with Gera, the elements of survival, determination and patience, are emphasized. When combined with Isa, this is an opportunity to recognize and accept your fate, see your part in what is happening in your life and face your fears.

Another aspect of Nauthiz, especially if this Rune shows up often in your life, is an indication of a life filled with need. Usually this is a misconception that life is hard, or that nothing comes easy, causing you to repeat patterns that cause distress, pain or confusion. Even in this case, Nauthiz is our friend, for it provides the power and will to overcome distress.

Element: Fire

Polairty: Rune of Balance

Color: Black, indicating the need to seek deep, inner wisdom. This color is sometimes connected to the Root Chakra. Since the Root Chakra is concerned with the lower back, sciatica, varicose veins, rectal bleeding, depression, immune disorders and osteoarthritis, if the Seeker has any of these physical ailments, the wisdom of this Rune can speak to those issues as well as emotional or spiritual issues.

Deity: Skuld, one of the Three Norns or Fates of Norse mythology. These are the spirits who sit beneath the World

Tree, Yggdrasil. Skuld is a goddess that represents things that are in the process of coming into being.

Universal Law: It may seem as if your needs are always just beyond your reach, but the source of all that you need comes from the Universe. If you are experiencing difficulties or are attracting experiences that hamper your movement, go "over the heads" so to speak, of those who are saying "no" and ask the Universe to intervene.

Reversed: The energy of Nauthiz in general and Nauthiz Reversed specifically is that of a teacher—not just any teacher but a Master teacher. Though the things that tend to come your way when Nauthiz energy is activated might seem difficult, remember that as long as you learn from your experiences, you have benefited from life's painful lessons.

The benevolent nature of Nauthiz Reversed is easier to see once you realize that in your moments of greatest darkness, you become aware of the resources hidden deep inside of you.

So when everything you do seems to fall apart, take time to reconsider what is important. Reorganize your life and your physical "stuff". Do a spring, summer, winter or fall cleaning. It doesn't matter where you start, just start!

If you have a habit of trying to control situations, lashing out in anger or giving in to impulses, take time to clear your inner self to make room for modesty and a good temper to grow.

Emotions: Discipline, constraint of freedom, too much hard work or drudgery when Upright. Distress, neediness, laziness, poverty, starvation, need, emotional hunger when Reversed.

Isa: Rune of the Contemplative Mind.

Isa is the Rune of quietness, standstill, withdrawal and icy stagnation. Times of your life when everything grinds to a halt can be "dark nights of the soul." A great thing about having a "dark night of the soul" is that it gives you the opportunity to dive deep into your own inner wisdom and find a quiet place to re-center and re-ground yourself.

If you feel like the lights that brightened your life path have suddenly gone out., look for the light deeper inside of yourself. Isa's energy is that of gestation or inner growth, like the hibernating bear that births her cubs in the coldest months of the year.

So you can see that Isa's stillness isn't really lack of motion, but an opportunity for deep, inner meditation. You know Isa's energy has entered your life when all your plans are suddenly on hold, or when you can't seem to muster up the energy to perform your normal daily tasks.

The sooner you recognize the pattern, the better, since trying make believe everything is "fine" and that life is going along as normal will only cause more emphasis on the Isa energy, creating a more pronounced stillness.

When Isa energy enters your life, the empty-handed leap of faith is calling. This means letting go of the aspects of your life where you feel that not doing or being a certain way will cause others to take you less seriously. In other words, center your energy on yourself and don't worry what anyone else thinks of you. This may seem like a huge sacrifice but this is the only thing that will bring on the thaw.

Isa might also offer a time out in the form of an illness, job loss or injury. Instead of stressing, take Isa's offered time-out to allow the restorative energies of the Universe to renew you at the deepest level. Read, meditate, do yoga, take a class. Remember that the Universe is in charge of the timing of your life.

You'll still be you even if you miss a few deadlines or change some of the ways you express yourself. Isa's energy has come to you because you are only seeing the "tip of the iceberg" so to speak, of the issues that need to change in your life. Because of this, Isa energy is the deepest form of patience.

The poise you will gain from the practice of deep focus and meditation will be well worth the temporary cold snap. Isa also strengthens the Runes around it, reinforcing their messages.

Element: Water, Ice

Color: Black, indicating the need for grounding in general and consideration of the Root and Earth Chakras. Since the Root Chakra is concerned with the lower back, sciatica, varicose veins, rectal bleeding, depression, immune disorders and osteoarthritis, if the Seeker has any of these physical ailments, the wisdom of this Rune can speak to those issues as well as emotional or spiritual issues.

Polarity: Rune of Balance

Deity: Verdandi. Verdandi is one of the Three Norns, or Weavers of destiny, that create fate in the moment. Verdandi is the present tense of the Old Norse verb, verda, meaning "to become" or "that which is happening/becoming."[22]

Universal Law: Times of stillness are normal and natural parts of life. When your life slows down, take the opportunity to deepen your spiritual path.

Merkstave: Isa has no reversed position but it can appear on its side, or Merkstave, in a Rune cast. If this is the case, the Isa energy can indicate a need for you to examine your life for any evidence of an ego on the rampage. On the other extreme, Isa Merkstave can indicate a dullness, blindness, or depression, as well as a tendency to be tricked by others or to trick or deceive others.

Emotions: Stillness, deep meditation, patience when Upright. Dullness, betrayal, guile, stealth, ambush, plots when Merkstave.

---

[22] http://en.wikipedia.org/wiki/Verdandi

Jera: Rune of Natural Cycles

The energy of Jera is that of abundance, the end result of hard work, the satisfaction from a job well done. If Jera has entered your life today, you can expect to reap the rewards and harvests of the plans you have nurtured over the past months or years.

Jera's appearance also announces a fertile season of your life. Some sources say the time frame of Jera is one year, others say it is a cycle or cycles of three. I like the cycle of three aspect because Jera speaks of times when people's lives were tied to the seasons and to the harvest cycles of crops. Most crops take three to six months to grow from seeds to mature plants, so the timeline of a year isn't necessarily what Jera is indicating.

I say not necessarily because one of the main energies behind the Rune Jera is that of patience. Whether you are being asked to wait three minutes, three days, three weeks or three months, you are being asked to exercise patience.

As a Rune of beneficial outcomes, Jera assures you that if you continue to tend your life garden, you absolutely will have a time of abundance. In the meanwhile, don't worry. You will complete your tasks and accomplish your goals at the best possible time. Jera is concerned with the Cosmic order, so its appearance in your life is validation that you are on the right track.

The cycles of Jera can also apply to cycles of life such as how childhood leads to adulthood, apprenticeship leads to mastery, etc. Remember that though you cannot act against the natural order, and that the natural order exists so that you will have a structure upon which to grow.

A Rune of peace and happiness, Jera assists you in breaking loose from times of stagnation. Specifically, Jera provides the perspective to remind you that you needn't worry about whether life will work out for you. Everything changes and grows in its own time. Don't forget that the greatest harvest of all, the harvest of the self, cannot fail.

Element: Earth

Color: Light blue, indicating the need to stabilize the energy of the Throat Chakra. Since the Throat Chakra is connected with sore throat, mouth ulcers, scoliosis, swollen glands, thyroid dysfunctions, tonsillitis, laryngitis, voice problems and gum or tooth issues, the wisdom of the Rune can speak to those issues as well as emotional or spiritual issues.

Polarity: Female

Deity: Freyja. Freyja, also known as Frigg or Frigga, is a major Norse goddess. She is said to be the wife of Odin, and as such, is the "foremost among the goddesses"[23] and the queen of Asgard. Freyja is a wife and mother figure in Norse mythological stories. She is also described as having the power of prophecy yet if she chooses to reveal anything at all, she does not reveal all of what she knows.

Frigg is described as the only one other than Odin who is permitted to sit on his high seat Hlidskjalf and look out over the universe, giving her a vast perspective. The English

---

[23] http://en.wikipedia.org/wiki/Freyja

term Friday derives from the Anglo-Saxon name for Frigg, Frige.

Universal Law: Patience and trust. All things are created in order to help us achieve our ultimate goal. The greatest harvest of all, the harvest of the Self, will occur no matter what.

Merkstave: Jera has no reverse, but if it appears in a Merkstave position, this can be a warning that you are attempting to go against the natural order and are making life harder than it needs to be. This can result in a sudden setback, a reversal of fortune, a failed business venture, a health challenge, or major change caused by bad timing.

These patterns can lead to poverty and inner and outer conflict. The remedy for this is to take a time out to look over your life in the past few months. Note where you have rushed the process, and reset your goals. If you are careful and aware, Jera's energy will lead you back to the path of abundance.

Emotions: Patience, sense of timing, balance and confidence when Upright. Impatience, rashness, frustration and confusion when Merkstave.

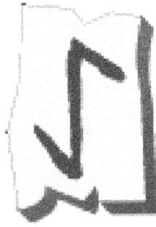

Eihwaz: The Rune of Defense and Experience

The energy of the Rune Eihwaz is that of defense, especially the kind of defense that comes from having the life experience and perspective to be able to see trouble before it arrives. Like a chess game where the players are able to see three or four moves ahead, Eihwaz offers the ability to be flexible enough have the power to defeat external or internal foes.

Eihwaz is also associated with the yew tree that has strong medicinal qualities that defend your health. The defensive qualities of the yew tree are so strong that it can turn around even deeply entrenched patterns of illness, stress, drama, emotional blindness or conditioning. Because of this, when Eihwaz comes into your life, consider your health.

If you are ill, Eihwaz offers strong support that can lead you to the sources you need to regain your health. If you are well, Eihwaz reinforces your efforts to maintain good health. Remember, the energy of Eihwaz is the strongest defensive power the Runes have to offer.

The wisdom that Eihwaz has to offer is that of patience. Instead of rushing ahead, slow down and consider your position. Perhaps if you wait, you will gain the upper hand.

If you are beginning a new phase in your life or a new venture, the energy of Eihwaz can support you in the delicate first steps by providing perseverance and foresight. If you feel as if you're stumbling around, meeting obstacles at every turn, this is the energy of Eihwaz urging you to calm down and center yourself.

Give yourself time to seek out more information. Once you have a clearer sense on the decision you need to make, decide, go forward without doubt or self-judgment.

Eihwaz speaks to one of the most powerful energy patterns in human life—the knife-edge combination of remarkable healing energy with the possibility of instant death due to toxicity. This speaks to your need for personal power yet the difficulty in wielding it well. Many famous people have felt the heavy weight of the pattern of Eihwaz—Marilyn Monroe, Michael Jackson, Judy Garland, and Karen Carpenter to name a few.

Eihwaz's energy might sound too risky until you consider the other side of the knife-edge—the possibility of enlightenment, due to the driving force to accomplish or create, the energy thread of purpose that runs through each life.

Since Eihwaz is concerned with the energy of life and death, and the cycles of life, when combined with Gera, Eihwaz asks you to consider where you are in your life. You are probably at a crossroads. So exercise patience, learn what you need to learn and then move forward with confidence.

Element: Metal. Some sources say the elements of Eihwaz are: earth, air, water and fire.

Polarity: Female

Color: Magenta. Magenta is sometimes associated with the Root Chakra. Since the Root Chakra is concerned with the lower back, sciatica, varicose veins, rectal bleeding, depression, immune disorders and osteoarthritis, if the

Seeker has any of these physical ailments, the wisdom of this Rune can speak to those issues as well as emotional or spiritual issues.

Deity: Ullr. Ullr is also called Urdl in the Old Norse. This god is associated with glory. Little is known of Urdl except for the reference to glory, but as we look at the energy of the Rune Eihwaz linked with the energy of glory, we can see that to move through the cycles of life with patience and in ways that engender peace and prosperity is a glorious thing, indeed.

Universal Message: Having the wisdom to defend yourself wisely requires patience and flexibility. When growth seems risky, remember that the Universe is limitless and contains all that you need.

Reversed: Eihwaz has no reverse but when it is in the Merkstave position, this can indicate a lack of defensive or protective energy in your life, leading to confusion, destruction, dissatisfaction, or weakness.

Eihwaz Merkstave can also indicate immaturity. Just because you're able to make things happen doesn't guarantee you have the wisdom and life experience to ride the wave or maintain the energy you've created in a way that is beneficial.

Eihwaz in the Merkstave position also speaks to health issues, specifically that you have not manifested enough defensive or protective measures to assure good health.

Emotions: Patience, perspective, vision, experience, excellent health and balance when Upright. Immaturity, confusion, dissatisfaction, blindness, sickness or weakness when Merkstave.

Perth: Rune of Initiation and Secrets

Perth is the energy of chance, like the Wheel of Fortune card of the Tarot. Perth's energy speaks to the uncertainties of the game of life. As such it is the Rune of initiation, specifically the kind of initiation into areas where the situation is unclear or not formed enough for you to be absolutely sure of your next step. Perth prefers that you move forward on faith and intuition, but it does let you know that powerful forces of change are working in your life.

Perth energy can bring you a sudden insight that gives you the courage to step forward or keep moving, even in areas where you'd given up hope. Perth is associated with the Phoenix, a sacred, mythical firebird spirit with colorful plumage and a golden tail. The Phoenix has a five hundred to one thousand year life cycle[24], at the end of which it builds itself a nest then self-ignites until both it and the nest are nothing but ashes. From the ashes a new, young Phoenix arises to live a new life that is as long as the old.

Perth's association with the phoenix reminds you that even when life seems to be burning all your bridges, so to speak, or taking so much that you're sure there will be nothing left, take heart. The old patterns are fading to make way for a new life and a new sense of self.

Though this can be an uncomfortable process, it is an important part of becoming whole. With the new energy

---

[24] http://en.wikipedia.org/wiki/Phoenix_(mythology)

and your willingness to risk come surprises and rewards. Perhaps you will surprise yourself by what you accomplish if you are challenged to restart your life from scratch.

Perhaps you have lost your job or have declared bankruptcy. Perth reminds you that these life changes are often a way to give you a fresh start. Perth challenges you to remember what you have already learned and to use discernment to guide your future choices.

As a mystery Rune, Perth grants you access to the inner secrets of the human world and the inner workings of nature. Perth teaches you to distinguish what is valuable and what is worthless.

As a yin energy Rune, Perth brings you back to the ultimate beginning, to the Womb of the great Goddess, Earth Mother Gaia. The mystery of Perth is that of Wyrd: that which continues to grow will continue to evolve, changing what is possible into reality and giving the perspective to see what may occur in the possibilities contained in the future.

The energy of Perth is strengthened when Odin appears in the same cast as this Rune, because both Perth and Odin are concerned with issues that are in the process of change or are still being created or formed.

Element: Water/yin

Color: Black, challenging us to look into areas where it is hard to see. Black is sometimes connected to the Root Chakra. Since the Root Chakra is concerned with the lower back, sciatica, varicose veins, rectal bleeding, depression, immune disorders and osteoarthritis, if the Seeker has any of these physical ailments, the wisdom of this Rune can speak to those issues as well as emotional or spiritual issues.

Polarity: Rune of Balance

Deity: Freyja. Freyja, also known as Frigg or Frigga is a major Norse goddess. She is said to be the wife of Odin. As such, she is the "foremost among the goddesses" and the queen of Asgard. Frigg appears as a wife and a mother in Norse mythologies. She is also described as having the power of prophecy, though she does not reveal what she knows. Frigg is the only one other than Odin who is permitted to sit on his high seat Hlidskjalf and look out over the universe. The English term Friday derives from the Anglo-Saxon name for Frigg, Frige.

Universal Law: Nothing is certain in this life. Forces of change are always in motion. If you risk, you could fail, but you can't win if you don't risk playing the game of life.

Reversed: Perth Reversed urges you to be cautious, patient and bide your time. Look over the projects you've started and see if and where you've become unfocused. Clarify your focus, even if it means giving up some of your pet projects.

Though others may be clamoring for your attention, you will benefit at this time from concentrating on your own life and what you need to do to grow. Instead of worrying about the future, or about deadlines and obligations, be present. Don't worry about what might or might not happen. Challenges and difficulties are gifts from the Universe to help you grow.

Perth Reversed indicates a possibility that you're ignoring or going against your own inner nature. The energy of Perth is a wake-up call to help you to see how to return to balance.

Emotions: Newness, wonder, rebirth, awe, and hope when Upright. Addiction, stagnation, loneliness, infertility, hastiness, failure and denial when Reversed.

Algiz: Rune of Protection and Personal Space

Algiz holds the most powerfully defensive energy of all the Runes. Algiz reminds you that it is possible and often necessary to form strong boundaries and protect yourself and your property, especially buildings and cars, without constantly fighting.

Algiz' protective energy can be compared to warnings like the rustle of grass, a rattlesnake's rattle or the antlers of a deer or elk. As such, it is concerned with keeping clear space around you and with the issue of boundaries. Setting boundaries doesn't mean pushing everyone away. Algiz's deepest protective powers are firm politeness and balance.

The most important thing to consider when Algiz energy enters your life is to keep your cool. If you need to create more personal space or set boundaries, doing so from a place of calm, clear emotional energy will be more helpful than simply shutting others out.

Algiz also speaks to times of change, challenge, new opportunities or transition in your life. Whenever you make changes, people will have various responses, from acceptance and respect to challenge to denial. Remember that you don't need anyone else's permission to set boundaries. Healthy boundaries allow positive energy to flow out to others and to flow in from others. The energy of Algiz isn't urging you to wall yourself off, just to clarify where you stand.

Because of the individualizing energy of Algiz, the energy behind this Rune can be called the mirror of the inner spiritual warrior. If others challenge you, remember that you are drawing that energy to you to help you confront your self. By standing your ground and standing up for yourself, you can win many battles without fighting. Right action and correct conduct are your only true protection.

Algiz also holds the power to help you focus your relationship with the Divine through the assistance of spirit helpers. The creating of personal boundaries has a tendency to challenge or even overturn the established order or hierarchy, similar to the Hierophant Reversed card of the Tarot.

Shield, sheltering self and others, follow your instincts.

Element: Air

Color: Gold, the color of protection from physical, emotional and energetic or psychic sources. Gold is sometimes associated with the Crown Chakra. Since the Crown Chakra is concerned with the physical issues of mystical depression, diseases of the muscle system, the skeletal system, the skin, chronic exhaustion, sensitivity to light, sound, environment, epilepsy and Alzheimer's disease, this Rune can speak to those issues as well as emotional or spiritual issues.

Polarity: Male

Deity: Heimdall. Heimdall is also spelled Hiemdallr. This Norse god has a horn that he blasts to herald major events. He rides the golden-maned horse Gulltoppr, has gold teeth and is the son of the Nine Mothers. Heimdall's main focus is that of the kind of precognitive knowledge that helps to avoid conflicts, pitfalls, disappointment and defeat.

Universal Law: No one can give you permission to exist. You have the right to your own personal space and to create boundaries. The Universe will defend you, no matter what.

Reversed: If Algiz Reversed appears in your life, consider your boundaries on all levels. This can include the hours you work, the people you associate with, what you eat and what you do in your free time. You may have created such strong boundaries that people who could be helpful aren't able to get close to you, or you could have allowed your boundaries to become so weak that harmful situations and people are entering.

Another consideration of Algiz Reversed is to be aware of your own health and energy levels. If your boundaries aren't strong, illness as well as other interfering influences can creep in.

No matter how desperately others seem to need you, remember that you can serve others better if you first care for yourself. You may need to set limits on what and when you're willing and able to give. It may sound selfish to consider yourself first but the real issue is to take responsibility for the position you have created for yourself in your life.

Remember, you have the right to turn away anyone or anything that you don't want in your space. If you don't create space for yourself, no one will do it for you. Don't worry about how things will work out. You may not always win but you will never lose if you learn from your experiences.

Emotions: Temperance, firmness, healthy boundaries, strong sense of self, politeness, clarity when Algiz appears upright. Weak boundaries, illness, lack of a sense of Divine connection, denial of your own right to exist, shunning, disinheritance when Reversed.

Sowelu: Rune of Immortality and Hope

Sowelu holds the energy of wholeness, life force and self-realization, which means a profound recognition of your true self. It is said that Narcissus' self-absorbed attitude evaporated when he accidentally saw his reflection in a pool and recognized the value of his true self. The moment he recognized his own energy, he ceased looking to others to validate him.

This profound recognition is the energy of Sowelu. It is the clear, focused energy of the absolute certainty of the life energy running through your life means that Sowelu's energy is that of the core path to individuality.

Sowelu embodies the culmination of the spiritual warrior's quest. The moment of self-recognition, similar to Narcissus' when you know without a doubt that what you have been beating your head against the wall, maybe for years, trying to become, is what you already are.

Sowelu energy is a conscious awakening that at once settles you and helps you to understand how to express your unique individuality in a creative way. Once you have recognized yourself, there will no longer be the tendency to tolerate stressful situations and people, nor will you be tempted to hide your true feelings in an effort to be polite.

You know you can simply choose to do something else, with someone else, which puts you in the driver's seat; a very energetically forward position. And if you've been reluctant about stepping forward and letting others know where you stand, Sowelu energy can help you to let your thoughts out into the light.

As you can probably see by now, Sowelu is a Rune of strength, like the sun itself. This Rune gives you the energy of the summer sun in full strength, so you can make powerful life changes.

Combined with Kano, Sowelu lights up your life path, giving a clear direction and evaporating the clouds or mist caused by mind games. With the aid of Sowelu's confident, optimistic energy, you can't lose! As you may have guessed, Sowelu is also the Rune of glowing health. This is partly because Sowelu's sword of flame makes it easier for you to see what you need to make your body/mind/spirit happy and what can be cleansed from your life.

As a sun Rune, Sowelu lifts you up into the atmosphere, making the contact between your higher self and unconscious, your spirit guides and helpers, more attainable.

Element: Fire.

Color: White, indicating a need to consider, clear, balance and fill the Crown Chakra. Since the Crown Chakra is concerned with the physical issues of mystical depression, which is a sadness over how this world is not living according to Universal Laws, diseases of the muscle system, the skeletal system, the skin, chronic exhaustion, sensitivity to light, sound, environment, epilepsy and Alzheimer's disease, this Rune can speak to those issues as well as emotional or spiritual issues.

Polarity: Rune of Balance

Deity: Baldur. Baldur is Odin's son, the Scandinavian God of Peace. He is a champion of goodness, innocence and forgiveness. Baldur's energy connection with Sowelu is that the more connected we are with our higher self, the more centered and peaceful we will be.

Universal Law: The core theme of life is self-realization. The greatest gift you can give to yourself is to be your whole self.

Merkstave: Sowelu has no reversed position, but if it shows up in your Rune cast on its side, or Merkstave, it is a warning that you may be putting on a false front. You may also be listening to bad advice, or in denial, trying to convince yourself that everything is really all right when your inner senses tell you that the opposite is the case.

The core issue here is that you aren't being true to your self. You may be enduring a relationship or partnership out of concern over hurting someone's feelings. You may be letting others make decisions for you. You may be relying on the success of someone else to feel good about yourself.

Whatever the issue is that is bringing out your false front, your gullibility is hurting you more than it's hurting anyone else. If you allow the light of Sowelu to show you the way back to your true self, all will be well. If not, you may lose everything, and by that I mean your sense of self-worth. The backlash may feel like the wrath of God raining down on your life.

Emotions: Confidence, clarity, justice, honesty, peace and forgiveness when upright. Gullibility, dishonesty, denial, immaturity and deceit if Merkstave.

Teiwaz: Rune of the Warrior and the Divinity in Humanity

The energy of Teiwaz is that of the warrior. Teiwaz reminds you that no matter what battles you are facing outside of your body/mind/spirit, the real battle is always with the self.

How do you fight the true battle then? By taking a good, honest look at yourself, including your motives and feelings. Then call upon the inner warrior to rise and fight the true battle as well as provide you with the weapons you need to succeed.

One of the weapons you can use is to become an observer. This means being unattached to outcomes. No matter what, even if it feels as if someone else is punching your buttons, remember that you are responsible for managing your own energy.

A deep study of yourself and your motives will increase your ability to discriminate, which helps you to know what you do and don't need. This deep inner study of yourself and this calling of your inner warrior take time, which is why Teiwaz counsels patience.

If you are sure that you are following Teiwaz' path, remember that you are in partnership with the Universe as well. The arrow like shape of Teiwaz reminds us that our supplications need to be focused on the Universe, not on people, groups or human organizations. Once you have done what you can do, wait for the Universe to make its move.

If Teiwaz has come into your life as a result of a relationship concern, this Rune indicates that the relationship is real. Move ahead with respect and care, not rushing into anything, and all will go well.

Your willingness to keep a cool head is a personal sacrifice, sometimes a challenging one to carry out, but letting go of drama gives you leverage to be a success. This is because giving up the little dramas of everyday life focuses positive energy into a clear intent.

As you can probably see, this approach works well in legal matters, when there is a human tendency to let stress push us around.

Element: Air

Color: Bright Red, indicating a need to focus on the Root Chakra. Since the Root Chakra is concerned with the lower back, sciatica, varicose veins, rectal bleeding, depression, immune disorders and osteoarthritis, if the Seeker has any of these physical ailments, the wisdom of this Rune can speak to those issues as well as emotional or spiritual issues.

Polarity: Male

Deity: Tiw, one of the oldest gods of the Germanic peoples. Tiw was concerned with the strategies and formalities of waging war. The emphasis on Tiw's energy is that of creating treaties, so there is a deep wisdom associated with this energy that transcends frontal attacks.

Universal Law: Diplomacy. The battle is never with outside forces. It is always with the self. Keep that in mind whenever you are facing conflict with others. Remember that inner peace creates outer peace.

Reversed: If Teiwaz appears in your life in a Reversed position, there is a good chance that you are letting things get to you. Whenever this happens, it's an indication that you need to calm down and refocus your intent.

If you don't, your energy is vulnerable and unstable. Other people will pick up on this and take advantage of you, possibly by cheating or manipulating you.

If you're feeling a bit off because a person you admire and appreciate is moving out of your life, remember that their presence or lack of presence in your life doesn't validate or invalidate you. Let people move in and out of your life as they need to. This gives you that same flexibility as well.

If you have betrayed a trust or someone has gossiped about you, remember that your battle is with yourself. If you are the gossiper, learn to be diplomatic. Apologize if need be. If you're the target of gossip, keep a cool head. Chuckle about it if you can and don't try to be in charge or dominate.

Emotions: Honor, justice, leadership, trust, authority, analysis, rationality when Upright. Betrayal, impatience, manipulation, sadness, control when Reversed.

Berkana: Rune of Growth and Rising Vibrations

Berkana is the Rune of growth, a rising spiral of energy that helps to raise your inner and outer vibrations. Berkana's season is spring, when rebirth and fertility surround us so completely that even those who live and work deep in manmade concrete jungles cannot be totally unaware of the cycle of blossoming and ripening.

If Berkana has entered your life today, this energy is urging you to clearly state what you do and do not want, because whatever you begin now will grow at a rapid pace.

This rapid growth can be a good thing, providing the things that are growing are things you really want. For example, if you are starting a business, be sure you really love what you are doing. If your business is expanding, don't hire someone unless they can do what you need them to do. If you were planting a garden, you wouldn't plant flowers that you were allergic to or that you don't like just to put something in the ground—would you?

Berkana also advises you that it's wise to remain calm and centered in this time of growth. Because any energy you fertilize at this time will grow, it's especially important to avoid drama. If stressful energy comes toward you, treat it from your calm center, with fairness, patience and generosity. Sometimes that generosity may take the form of having to say "no." Why is a denial generous? It's generous because you are providing a life lesson.

Remember, you are creating this growth, so no one has the right to take it from you or decide for you how to use it.

You are being fed directly from the breasts of the Earth Mother, Gaia, so keep your motives pure and don't act needy or anxious, especially if this time of new growth has come to you after a long, cold wintry spell.

Berkana is a powerful feminine Rune, since it has to do with the energy of fertility, growth and bearing fruit. You have the opportunity not only to finish longstanding projects to make room for something new, but the new things you start will have a higher vibrational level. This is why it's so important to be sure that what you are growing, an attitude, business, relationship or project, is what you really want to grow.

Berkana is associated with the number eighteen, which is double the sacred nine. Berkana holds the energy of awakening and the arousal of desire. When combined with Fehu, Berkana's energy is that of prosperity and success in business matters.

Element: Earth.

Color: Dark green, indicating the need to focus on the energies of the Heart Chakra. Since the Heart Chakra is concerned with heart conditions, asthma, lung and breast cancers, middle (thoracic) spine, pneumonia, upper back, shoulder and high blood pressure, if the Seeker has any of these physical issues, the wisdom of this Rune can speak to those issues as well as emotional or spiritual issues.

Polarity: Female

Deities: Nerthus, the goddess associated with fertility, peace and wealth. Nerthus may have been hermaphroditic, having the energies of both male and female. In ancient

Denmark, her image was carried around on a sacred, covered wagon to herald the arrival of spring.

Holda: Also spelled Holle, an aspect of the Earth Mother or Gaia. Holda is the Matron of spinning, childbirth, domestic animals and interestingly enough, is also associated with winter, witches and the Wild Hunt. Just as the elements of the natural world are diverse, dovetailing one into another, so Holda reminds us that there are pleasant and difficult aspects associated with growth and giving birth. Holda has a helpful disposition and isn't easily irritated unless she discovers sloppy upkeep in household affairs.

Universal Law: Responsibility and clarity. Be careful what you choose to grow, as anything, even a negative or angry attitude, will grow for you at this time.

Reversed: Berkana Reversed sends you the message that there is something interfering with your growth. This can be anything from being too easygoing and allowing people to cross your boundaries to self-sabotage. To turn this around, go over the events of the past weeks or months. Think through any areas where you may be putting your needs before the needs of others, or where you are allowing others to use you. Be flexible and nonjudgmental as you consider your options and make changes.

Emotions: Clarity, control of emotions, fertility, fairness, patience prosperity and generosity when Upright. Family, business or other relationship problems, anxiety, carelessness, abandon, loss of control, blurring of consciousness, deceit, sterility and stagnation when Reversed.

Ehwaz: Rune of Movement and the Unbreakable Bond

Ehwaz offers the energy of steady, forward movement and incremental progress toward a goal. Ehwaz is also the Rune of transportation, physical or energetic shifts, new homes and new attitudes that can give you the energy to create a new life. Ehwaz is the sense of stability and accomplishment you feel when you realize that you have enough life experience to have a stable position in life, and a large enough financial and energetic base to share your good fortune and wisdom with others.

If Ehwaz has entered your life today, it is offering the energy to improve a difficult situation. Perhaps a misunderstanding can be cleared up or an opportunity that has been closed to you will open up. This is partly due to the fact that Ehwaz provides you with the energy to form a serious enough intention to carry your plans forward to completion.

Ehwaz energy is connected to the energy of the horse. Horses were considered sacred animals because they carried Gods and Goddesses. The idea here is that a horse and rider were partnered for life, indicating that you are sure enough about how life works to create and enjoy lasting relationships on all levels.

The aspect of enduring partnerships is strengthened when Ehwaz is combined with Gebo. When combined with Wunjo, Ehwaz provides the energy to create and/or maintain an ideal marriage.

The idea of an optimal, lasting partnership implies the need for trust. Not just the idea of trust or the striving for trust, but absolute trust and loyalty that transcends human loyalties and anchors itself in the Universal Laws of Love and Light.

Element: Air.

Color: White, indicating the need for balance, clearing or other consideration of the Crown Chakra. Since the Crown Chakra is concerned with the physical issues of mystical depression, diseases of the muscle system, the skeletal system, the skin, chronic exhaustion, sensitivity to light, sound, environment, epilepsy and Alzheimer's disease, this Rune can speak to those issues as well as emotional or spiritual issues.

Polarity: Male

Deity: Freyja. Freyja, also known as Frrigg or Frigga is a major Norse goddess. She is said to be the wife of Odin and is the "foremost among the goddesses" as well as the queen of Asgard. Frigg appears primarily in Norse mythological stories as a wife and a mother. She is also described as having the power of prophecy yet she keeps to herself what she knows. Frigg is described as the only one other than Odin who is permitted to sit on his high seat Hlidskjalf and look out over the universe. The English term Friday derives from the Anglo-Saxon name for Frigg.

Universal Law: Movement and growth are normal and necessary parts of life. Change may sometimes be challenging, but it is the energy of stagnation that builds enough pressure to create the forward movement. No one can take from you what is really yours.

Reversed: Ehwaz Reversed is the energy of treading water. You're moving, but you aren't getting anywhere. In fact, your movements are creating a lot of unwanted attention and leaving you exhausted.

To open this blockage, stop thrashing. Think through the opportunities you have available. Even if, at this point, you need to choose the lesser of the evils, make a decision and stick to it. If it seems that you can't choose without losing something, remember, no one can take from you what is really yours.

Emotions: Steady forward movement, growth, ability to change, balance, harmony and peace when Upright. Restlessness, blockage, recklessness, disharmony, mistrust and betrayal when Reversed.

Mannez: Rune of the Self and of the Source

Mannez is the energy of core issues; the starting point, which is why some Rune masters place Mannez as the first Rune. Mannez reminds you of the importance of having a healthy, balanced relationship with yourself. As you may imagine, Mannez' appearance in your life can signal a time of inner reflection that leads to growth.

There are times in your life when you may just want to get on with it, but you won't get far if you don't know yourself well enough to be sure you can handle what is coming to you.

Mannez reminds you that you don't need to feel rushed or stressed. Just do your tasks for no reason other than to add your own unique presence to that task. Remember, hidden within the mundane daily tasks is the core of joy for your life. And, if you divide Mannez down the center, you will create mirror images of Wunjo, the Rune of Joy.

If you feel alone, as if you have no one to lean on, consider Mannez. The two Wunjo shapes that create this Rune support each other, reminding you that it is the self that balances and supports the self. In other words, when your inner world is at peace with the outer world, your life will be in balance.

So, live your life without judgment. Be available and receptive to the Divine presence of your Higher Self and your Spirit Guides.

Mannez also reminds you to be aware of the cyclical nature of life—the rise and fall of growth cycles. Each cycle follows the other in its order. Mannez gives you the energy to accept this and also to set right any aspects of your life that have slipped out of balance.

Basic human qualities, shared life experiences, social order, stability, communication, gaining advantage in disputes and tests.

Mannez is also connected to the elements of the Tree of Life. There is a Scandinavian legend that says that the first humans were made from trees. Mannez can also provide insight into contracts or agreements between men and women.

If Mannez has entered your life at a time when you feel alone, don't despair—if you look you will find help and/or cooperation with others now.

Element: Water

Color: Deep red, indicating a need to consider your Root Chakra. Since the Root Chakra is concerned with the lower back, sciatica, varicose veins, rectal bleeding, depression, immune disorders and osteoarthritis, if the Seeker has any of these physical ailments, the wisdom of this Rune can speak to those issues as well as emotional or spiritual issues.

Polarity: Rune of Balance

Deities: Heimdall. Heimdall is the god of the resounding horn. Heimdall's energy is that of charging forward, riding his golden-maned horse, Gulltoppr. His appearance can be sudden and his light startling. He has a strong sense of foreknowledge and sharp hearing and eyesight. His motives are so pure that he is known as "the whitest of the gods."

Odin. Odin is one of the primary Norse gods, considered by some sources to be a shape shifter.[25] Odin is considered to be a leader of souls, though the direction he chooses to lead may not be as clear as we may prefer. Odin is often depicted on horseback, holding a spear in one hand and accompanied by a raven.

Frigg, also known as Freyja or Frigga is a major Norse goddess. She is said to be the wife of Odin and is the "foremost among the goddesses" as well as the queen of Asgard. Frigg appears primarily in Norse mythological stories as a wife and a mother. She is also described as having the power of prophecy yet she keeps to herself what she knows. Frigg is described as the only one other than Odin who is permitted to sit on his high seat Hlidskjalf and look out over the universe. The English term Friday derives from the Anglo-Saxon name for Frigg.

Universal Message: You are a unique individual and are well-loved by the Universe.

Reversed: Mannez reversed reminds you to be clear with yourself and not to discount yourself. If Mannez Reversed has come into your life today, consider carefully: Are you deceiving yourself?

Mannez Reversed can cancel out or counteract other Runes, so take careful note of its placement in a Rune Cast. If your are allowing the opinions and expectations of others to cause you to feel confused, remember that ultimately, the person you need to make happy is yourself. This means learning to recognize, rely on and follow your inner wisdom and intuition.

---

[25] http://en.wikipedia.org/wiki/Odin

You can discover your own inner voice by finding quiet time to meditate. Remember, outer stresses and events are reflections of your inner disturbances. You can reclaim your balance by recognizing the damage that your self-sabotaging habits are having and stopping the cycle.

If the idea of starting over leaves you feeling frustrated, remember that you are always at the beginning and that no matter how many plans you create, the present is all you have.

Emotions: Modesty, devotion, moderation, knowledge, wisdom, patience and intellectual strength when Upright. Depression, mortality, blindness, self-delusion, cunning, slyness, manipulation and isolation when Reversed.

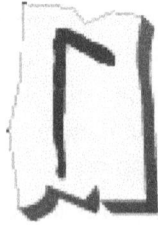

Laguz: Rune of Flow and Abundant Life Force

Laguz is the Rune of the rising and falling of the tides of life, the flow of life energy and of water. Just as only the tip of an iceberg can be seen, Laguz reminds you that there are hidden powers that nourish, shape or connect your life.

Laguz' energy is concerned with flow of all kinds: emotions, careers, relationships, plans and life cycles. Laguz urges you to immerse yourself in living without judging or scrutinizing yourself or others. Laguz wakes you up to the presence of your intuitive or lunar nature that flows in harmony with the Universe itself.

If Laguz has entered your life today, this may be a signal that it is a good time to reorganize your life. You can start the process by physically cleaning up your home and work space, or by beginning a practice of meditation to encourage a deeper knowing of what makes your life energies flow.

Laguz also urges you to study spiritual subjects in preparation for self-transformation. It is sometimes called the happily ever after Rune because it brings you to the place of what alchemists call the conjunctio[26] or sacred marriage, where you have worked through your life challenges and will now be able to leave many of the distressing energies of life behind.

When you consider the energies that make your life flow, consider the power of the ocean tides or the force of a waterfall that has the energy to create electricity or clear

---

[26] Blum, Ralph, The Book of Runes, p. 127.

logjams and other blockages. If you move with the flow of energy of your life, you will have less of a challenge removing the blockages from your path and be cleaned and refreshed as well.

Laguz reminds you to swim with the flow of energy presented in your life. If you try to swim against the current, you will struggle and be thrown about. You can't live for long without water but you can't live for long in water, either.

When combined with Gera, Laguz reminds us that all growth comes in cycles, in its own time. Even if there are emotional storms around you, your calm, inner flow can reflect a calm energy to remind you that there are blue skies above.

When combined with Raido, Laguz can indicate success in travel.

Element: Water

Color: Dark Green, indicating a need to consider, balance or clear the Heart Chakra. Since the Heart Chakra is concerned with heart conditions, asthma, lung and breast cancers, middle (thoracic) spine, pneumonia, upper back, shoulder and high blood pressure, if the Seeker has any of these physical issues, the wisdom of this Rune can speak to those issues as well as emotional or spiritual issues.

Polarity: Female

Deity: Njord, father of the deities Freyja and Freyr. Njord is associated with the sea, sea voyages, the wind, fishing, wealth and crop fertility.

Universal Law: Flexibility will bless you by helping you ride what may be rough waves for some, and by helping you discover your own inner music.

Reversed: If Laguz Reversed has entered your life today, you may be trying to go against the natural flow of your life. Take a time out and consider how you've been acting. Have you been ignoring your health, for example, by eating too much fast food?

Laguz Reversed reminds you that though you have a spark of Divinity at your core, you are still human. Make an effort to get enough sleep, exercise and healthy food. If you aren't able to go with the flow in one area, find an area where you can. Draw on Universal wisdom by consulting your intuitive side.

Emotions: The currents of life, creativity, fertility, flexibility, dreams, fantasies, psychic intuition, inner power and the ability to remove blockages when Upright. A time of confusion due to wrong decisions or judgments, lack of creativity, drought, feelings of being in a rut, fear, circular motion like a whirlpool, avoidance, withering, madness, obsession, despair, perversity, sickness, suicide, when Reversed.

Inguz: Rune of the Beacon of Light

Inguz' energy is concerned with fertility, new beginnings and intuitive energy, which links it to the new moon. Inguz' double "X" shape indicates the presence of empowering energy that gives you the strength and balance to finish the projects that you start.

In fact, follow-through is an important aspect of Inguz energy. If Inguz has entered your life today, you can expect greater harmony and balance in relationships. If you've been struggling with snarled communication or setbacks, Inguz brings the issues to light in your favor, creating satisfaction for all involved, or at least, causing any troublesome person or persons to decide that there is no reason to fight with you.

Inguz often appears at the beginning of new projects, new life, new relationships, or new jobs. As you create and complete projects, you fertilize the environment around you, which benefits yourself and others.

The energy of Inguz gives you the sense of inner strength and confidence that allows parts of yourself to come out into the light that you haven't felt confident enough in before, freeing you from tension and uncertainty.

Since Inguz is concerned with fertility, this Rune sends strong messages to your intimate relationships and toward any gardening or landscaping projects you may be beginning, planning or maintaining. If you have a special someone, the energy of Inguz sparks your inner kundalini fire, igniting your passion. If you are an avid gardener, Inguz can help you to choose what, when and where to plant your flowers and plants.

Since Inguz reminds you of the support available to you from the Universe, there is a sense of the limitless expansion of the Universe in your life at this moment. This carries your inner energy outward, allowing you to share your light far and wide.

When combined with Thurisaz, the Gateway Rune, or Isa, Rune of Stillness, Inguz speaks of the deep, meditative resting phase that often come before internal growth, rest stage. This is a place of deep, inner calm without anxiety. You know that any loose ends will be tied up and accounted for without causing any stress in your life. You are now free to move in a new direction.

Elements: Water and earth

Polarity: Female

Color: Yellow, indicating that contemplation is advised on the Solar Plexus Chakra. Since the Solar Plexus Chakra is connected to stomach ulcers, intestinal tumors, diabetes, pancreatitis, indigestion, anorexia/bulimia and hepatitis, the wisdom of this Rune can speak to those issues as well as emotional and spiritual issues.

Deity: Ing, the Hero God. Ing is also called the God of Fertility. Ing was the male consort of the Earth Mother, Gaia. As the God of male fertility and nurture, Ing is also the protector of house, hearth and family. His support was an assurance of good hunting and a bountiful harvest. He also represented the healthy and productive side of sexuality. Ing is the power and influence of the earth.

Universal Law: Balance and harmony is achieved when we are able to dive into our inner wisdom and use that to inform our outward actions.

Merkstave: Inguz has no Reversed position, but when it turns up sideways, or Merkstave, it can indicate that you are treading water—making a lot of motions without creating growth or change. You may be wandering around without a clear goal or creating work for yourself due to an unfocused or careless state of mind. This sharply reduces your clarity and effectiveness.

To alleviate this pattern, consult your inner wisdom and ask for guidance form the Universe. Take a time-out to think through your present position. What are your options? What can you change to make your life run more smoothly? What do you need to give up? Which parts of yourself are you keeping hidden away that need to be expressed?

Once you know what you would like to change, move into the changes and feel your self-confidence growing and your inner energy stabilize.

Emotions: Creativity, fertility, co-creation, growth, success and balance when Upright. Confusion, wasted time, frustration when Merkstave.

Dagaz: Rune of Transformation

Dagaz is the Rune of breakthrough and transformation that helps you to rise to a higher vibration. In short, Dagaz energy is sun energy, the energy of the day. If Dagaz has entered your life today, this can signal a major shift or breakthrough in your life that can change the way you see life forever.

This change can manifest as a new job, a change of heart or a new perspective. Since the main focus of the Runes is the process of self-change, the inner changes in mood or attitude are seen as more valuable than the outer manifestations. This is because the inner changes generate the outer changes that are recognizable to most people as hard evidence, such as successes, career changes or money matters.

This power of change is especially helpful because it is driven by your own inner sun and directed by your own will.

If you've been struggling with a person or issue, for example, the energy of Dagaz can cause you to completely shift your point of view at just the right time, so that you are no longer struggling. This can come as a sudden insight that is so timely that if you recognize and seize the opportunity, your life will change forever.

Dagaz can also indicate a major period of achievement and prosperity. The sun is shining in your life, pushing the darkness far behind you.

How Dagaz helps you to have energetic breakthroughs is at once simple and profound. It brings you to a balance at the right time and place, to the zero-point of contact with the Universe. This balance between polar opposites gives you a profound perspective that can give you the leverage to resolve almost any conflict.

Dagaz energy is also concerned with the mid-points in life. From the middle of the day, meaning lunch meetings, messages received in the middle of the day, to seasons such as midsummer, as well as other high points of the day, year and of your life itself. Dagaz points to times of strength and well being, to the rise and fall of life cycles, and to the type of closure that creates space for more openness.

Dagaz also strengthens your warrior nature, giving you the energy to be yourself without concerns about whether other people will like you or agree with you.

Dagaz also has one other interesting and unique aspect. When it appears beside, above or below the Odin Rune, Dagaz can indicate a death. I've had this combination come up and each time there has been either a recent or impending physical death, or the death of an idea, a huge, shocking dis-illusionment that, once the moment of dismay has passed, turns out to be a benefit to the individual.

Even the death aspect of the Dagaz/Odin combination isn't meant to be negative or sad, because this combination indicates a successful, timely passing to the next plane of existence. This can bring meaning to what may seem like a senseless or early death by providing the perspective that though we may have wanted the person to remain on Earth longer, that this truly was their time to go.

Dagaz also offers protective power, especially when combined with Thurisaz, Algiz or Teiwaz.

When combined with Kano, Dagaz provides opening space for new ideas to form. Dagaz can stop harmful people or energies from entering your space and your boundaries when combined with Eihwaz or Othila, without blocking the things we need.

When combined with Berkana, Dagaz provides security and growth, releasing you from old conditioning and patterns that aren't helpful to you.

Elements: Fire and Air

Color: Light blue, indicating focus is needed on the Throat Chakra. Since the Throat Chakra is connected with sore throat, mouth ulcers, scoliosis, swollen glands, thyroid dysfunctions, tonsillitis, laryngitis, voice problems and gum or tooth issues, the wisdom of the Rune can speak to those issues as well as emotional or spiritual issues.

Dagaz is also associated with the Third Eye Chakra. Since the Third Eye Chakra is concerned with brain tumors, strokes, blindness, deafness, seizures and learning disabilities, this Rune can speak to these issues as well as emotional and spiritual issues.

Polarity: Male

Deity: Heimdall. Heimdall is the god of the resounding horn. Heimdall's energy is that of charging forward, riding his golden-maned horse, Gulltoppr. His appearance can be sudden and his light startling. He has a strong sense of foreknowledge and sharp hearing and eyesight. His motives are so pure that he is known as "the whitest of the gods."

Universal Law: Transformation and enlightenment are powerful aspects of life that everyone can benefit from.

Merkstave: Dagaz has no Reversed position, but when it appears in your life on its side, or Merkstave, it can indicate that your energies are focused too much on competing with others instead of on the present moment, which could limit what you can do and the influence you can wield in the world.

The energy of competition is a limiting energy, one that is focused on the idea that ether isn't enough for everyone, so someone has to "win" and someone has to "lose." Be careful with this energy, as any limits you enforce may end up limiting you. The energy of competition can also create blindness to anything other than your own goals, which can cause endings and misunderstandings in relationships.

To turn this cycle around, widen your perspective. Let the sun shine on all of your life, illuminating your motives even in your most private areas. Even though you may intend that no one know your deepest worries and fears, they manifest themselves through your actions. So in that way, they aren't secret at all.

Emotions: Success, strength, excellent health, breakthroughs, positive changes, permanent changes for the good, balance and harmony when Upright. Competition, blindness, limits, tiredness and poor health when Merkstave.

Othila: Rune of Energetic Fences

Othila is concerned with the energy of boundaries. Though energetic fences may be invisible, they can be clearly felt, so are an effective way to create healthy boundaries. Boundary-setting needs to be done with care, since setting even the friendliest boundaries still involve separation on some level.

The kinds of separation created by healthy boundaries are usually behavior-related, and as such are really issues of respect. For example, if you prefer that people don't smoke in your home, you might choose to place a sign on your front door that says, "No smoking." If someone chooses to smoke anyway, you can choose not to invite them to your home again.

Often, as we are considering how and where to create a boundary, we must first decide what the boundary is for. This means separating out or retreating from areas where we may have chosen to be in the past.

Clarity and objectivity are essential here, as some boundaries may go against ideas about a sense of self that have been inherited from past familiar patterns. For example, if you have been told all your life that you don't have the right to have an opinion, setting boundaries might be challenging for you. But until you begin to set boundaries, people don't have a sense of who you are.

Sure, some people might choose not to be your friend once they scope out your boundaries but it's not only kinder to allow others to clearly see who you are, it's also healthier for you.

If Othila has come into your life today, you might face challenges to step more firmly into your adulthood. Creating boundaries usually creates a more sharply defined sense of individuality, which also creates a separation between the adult you and the remnants of the child you.

Because of the separation aspects of Othila, you might lose bits of yourself, but they will be bits that you are finished with, like a snake shedding its skin. On a Universal level, there is also an aspect of submission attached to Othila's message, but not the kind of submission that says, "Oh, well, I've been under the dogpile this long, I may as well stay here."

The submission contained in Othila's message is that of recognizing what the Laws of the Universe are and how they work. For example, since balance and harmony are Universal Laws, the role of scapegoat goes against those Laws. So the submission aspect is to submit to the Universal Laws even if that means risking losing a human contact or contacts.

The setting of boundaries can also indicate a need for withdrawal on your part, helping you to choose which relationships are healthiest for you. Establishing strong, healthy boundaries can open the doors to blessings, rewards and benefits by strengthening your inner sense of self.

Othila's energy also speaks to the kinds of inheritance that come from something you must give up. If you have allowed yourself to be the family scapegoat, for example, your ability to shed your attachment to that identity will be a blessing to you for the rest of your life. Othila asks you to consider how you can become more of who you truly are.

While physical inheritances can be a part of this Rune's energy, Othila's main concern is on energetic inheritances and inner strength that no one can take from you.

Remember, no one can steal your soul no matter how much damage you suffer. It is your right to create and maintain boundaries and pass down the rights and privileges of personal boundaries from to your children and grandchildren. Your sacred inner space is an enclosure that cannot be taken away.

No matter what kind of car you drive, how big or fancy your house is or how many clothes you have, your sacred inner space is your true wealth.

When combined with Raido Reversed, Othila can indicate communication challenges and the need for clearer boundaries on your part.

Element: Earth

Color: Deep yellow, indicating the need to focus on or consider the Solar Plexus Chakra. Since the Solar Plexus Chakra is connected to stomach ulcers, intestinal tumors, diabetes, pancreatitis, indigestion, anorexia/bulimia and hepatitis, the wisdom of this Rune can speak to those issues as well as emotional and spiritual issues.

Polarity: Male

Deity: Odin. Odin is one of the primary Norse gods, considered by some sources to be a shape shifter.[27] Odin is considered to be a leader of souls, though the direction he chooses to lead may not be as clear as we may prefer. Odin is often depicted on horseback, holding a spear in one hand and accompanied by a raven. Othila indicates the need for strong boundaries and even separation from people, ideas

---

[27] http://en.wikipedia.org/wiki/Odin

and/or places that are familiar or held dear. It's no wonder that Odin is associated with this Rune.

Universal Message: Having strong boundaries is a healthy habit that can help you to feel safe and secure in your life path.

Reversed: Othila Reversed indicates a need to free yourself from old or ill-fitting conditioning and distance yourself from old authority figures or structures. Failure to stand up for who you are can cause pain to others and yourself.

If Othila Reversed has entered your life today, it is challenging you to cultivate your inner spaces and be willing to adapt with a sense of inner entitlement and skill. When you have done all you can, send your concerns to the Universe and wait for the Universe to act. You may be letting your anger rule you or letting others push you around. Remember, you have all the answers you need inside of you.

Emotions: Boundaries, justice, sacred space, sense of being home, security and confidence when Upright. Abandonment, totalitarianism, slavery, poverty, prejudice and polarization when Reversed.

Odin: Rune of the Void--Rune of
Unlimited Potential

Odin is the blank Rune; the symbol-less symbol. The beginning. The end. The All-Father. The Divine. The Rune of total trust. A circle of space that is at once the physical you and the Divine you, with arrows pointing out in all directions.

If Odin has entered your life today, you are in contact with your own true destiny. As an energy of ending, Odin can indicate a death—though this death is usually symbolic. What you are being asked to do is to relinquish control, let go and trust.

Remember that Odin's blankness holds undiluted potential; the totality of your being and the Being of the Universe Itself. Odin asks you to look into the Void and face your deepest fears.

Not only fear, but all your hopes and dreams lie here. Many people spend their lives inventing ways to avoid looking into the Void. Again and again you are brought to the place where you have the opportunity to jump into the empty space with nothing except your sense of self.

Odin also reminds you that karma is not a debt that you came into life with that you must pay. Karma shifts and changes moment to moment, as you shift and evolve. Nothing is predestined. Do you see the power in this Rune? Do you see the level of confidence that the Universe has placed in you? Next time you feel as if you need someone to believe in you, think about the message of Odin's Rune and remember how much the Universe believes in you.

Anything is possible. Just choose a direction and go for it. Your life is a blank page. Start writing your life as you want it to be.

Odin also reminds you that many parts of life are beyond your control. In those moments when you feel like life is spinning out of control, look to the Universe and you will find threads of your current life that are in the process or ending and other threads that are in the process of forming. If you focus on this process instead of the current stress or pain, you will gain the perspective to see yourself as part of the Whole.

Odin reminds you that often when you feel the most empty is when life asks you to leap into the Void. The Void itself is often misunderstood to be the ultimate scary place, a place of monsters or demons that is detached from your personal life. The ultimate Void is your deepest self. So what is there to fear? What Odin is really challenging you to do is to trust more in your own inner wisdom and to dive more deeply into your own hidden self.

You are in control of you.

Element: Air

Color: Runic Blue, indicating a need to focus on the Throat Chakra. Since the Throat Chakra is connected with sore throat, mouth ulcers, scoliosis, swollen glands, thyroid dysfunctions, tonsillitis, laryngitis, voice problems and gum or tooth issues, the wisdom of the Rune can speak to those issues as well as emotional or spiritual issues.

The Blank Rune is also connected to the Third Eye Chakra. Since the Third Eye Chakra is concerned with brain tumors, strokes, blindness, deafness, seizures and learning disabilities, this Rune can speak to these issues as well as emotional and spiritual issues.

Polarity: Rune of Balance

Deity: Odin. Odin is one of the primary Norse gods, considered by some sources to be a shape shifter.[28] Odin is considered to be a leader of souls, though the direction he chooses to lead may not be as clear as we may prefer. Odin is often depicted on horseback, holding a spear in one hand and accompanied by a raven.

Universal Law: Be here now. There is no past. There is no future. All that you really have is now. Many people don't live in the now because the present moment contains so much mystery and uncertainty. Yet, it is all we have. This moment is the time when we can prove that we don't deserve to carry the karma of the past.

Odin Reversed: The Blank Rune has no reverse and no Merkstave position. No matter where it appears in a Rune cast, its messages and challenges remain the same.

Emotions: Trust, presence, potential, self-worth, karma, vulnerability.

---

[28] http://en.wikipedia.org/wiki/Odin

Chapter 15:

Meanings of Heart Runes

Heart Runes use the same basic meanings in a Heart Rune cast as in any other cast, but the focus is slightly different.

This chapter lists each Rune and gives the Heart Rune meaning for each. I use only the Upright meanings of the Runes for Heart Runes because they contain the overall essence of the energy contained in each Rune.

Fehu

Fehu is the Rune of Fulfillment. Drawing Fehu indicates that your life path is on an upward or rising spiral. This is not just a blessing, but the energy of blessings pressed down, as in compressing material to fit inside of a bag; in other words, huge, overflowing, exuberant blessings.

Fehu is concerned with the kind of wealth that, once created, continues to recreate itself. This indicates that people with Fehu as a heart Rune have a knack of finding ways to make money or attain personal growth through systems or developing new methods of thinking that become like a perpetual motion machine. Paired with Inguz, this indicates that your intuition plays a big part in what you develop.

Fehu as a Heart Rune indicates that your Root and Heart Chakras are strong, open and secure. Your sense of selfhood and existence are firmly rooted in the Universe, beyond the reach of human politics and mind games. This allows you to express your big, open heart to everyone you care about.

Fehu also asks you to think deeply about what profit and gain will mean for you in this lifetime. What will you use your energy for—wealth for wealth's sake or a balance of inner and outer wealth? Fehu also implies that you have a strong and stable sense of self-worth. No one needs to tell you that you are a unique person with value, though you may like to be reminded of that.

A life challenge for people with Fehu as a Heart Rune is

to refrain from doing "for" people. It's so easy for you to figure out how to care for yourself that you can become snarled in other people's troubles. Remember that just as the Universe has given you what you need to make your way in this world, so has the Universe given others the inner and outer resources that they need.

If others haven't figured out how to have the physical resources that they need, what they really need is to recognize their inner worth and learn to utilize their inner resources. You can inspire them, but if you do too much for them, not only will you tax your own energy but you will enable them to continue feeling as if they can't create outer wealth.

Another challenge from Fehu is to share your good fortune appropriately with others. This means giving when you have extra but more often means helping to instill in others the deep belief in their sense of self.

Uruz

Uruz is the Rune of strength and self-empowerment, of beginnings and endings, of what it means to be a man or a woman at this time and place.

If you have Uruz as a Heart Rune, this indicates that you are strong enough to take on the challenges and changes in life. Your Sacral Chakra is strong, which means you're able to create new beginnings, including but not limited to projects, relationships, businesses and friendships.

The strength of Uruz also gives you the ability to create endings where needed, without feeling as if you're a failure. Even if you need to terminate a long-term, precious relationship, you know the timing is right. Uruz gives you a good sense of the temporary nature of mortal life as well as providing the strength to begin again. Because of these factors, your sense of hope never dies. You know that each ending creates the space for a new beginning.

Having Uruz as a Heart Rune gives you the ability to tolerate the temporary disruption that occurs when your life is in the process of reorganizing. People with Uruz as a Heart Rune have the perspective to see the big picture. Everything has its place and for something new to grow, something old often dies and sometimes provides the fertile ground for the new.

Part of Uruz' strength is knowing that lasting, authentic change can never be forced. Discernment—the ability to see an opportunity disguised as a loss and the ability to see the strengths in the male and female spirit, gives Uruz people the ability to handle heavy loads, though they resist times when they feel they are being forced or manipulated into using their strength.

Uruz people are good, willing helpers but are strongly independent and prefer to cooperate as an equal partner rather than submit. Like the wild ox that Uruz is associated with, it is wise if others appreciate and respect the strength of an Uruz person.

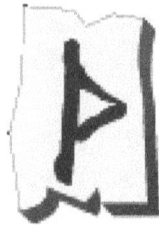

Thurisaz

If Thurisaz is your Heart Rune, you may feel that you are at a crossroads over and over again. Just as you get used to one pattern of life, the pattern changes and you end up at a place where you need to make a tough decision yet again.

The key to claiming the greatest benefit of having Thurisaz as your Heart Rune is to develop a broad, Universal perspective. Remember that the lessons you learn in this particular life may be penetrating and sometimes sharp, that you can use the wisdom that you gain from these lessons to raise your vibration and to climb to a different place.

In fact, this is the core of the challenge of Thurisaz as a Heart Rune. As you continue to cross into gateway after gateway, you grow and develop quickly. Each time you approach a new gateway, take a few minutes to think back over your past life.

Let the images of your life flow through your body/mind/spirit freely, without judgment. Send a blessing to each of them, and then release them. As you feel the energy flowing through you, cleansing you like a breeze on a spring day, take a deep breath, turn your attention back to the new gateway, and step through once again.

Thurisaz is connected to the Root and Sacral Chakras, giving foundational energy to your life. Thurisaz takes you back to the beginning, necessitating that you are constantly releasing old energy so that you are ready to create something new, while reminding you that no matter what, your place in the Universe is secure.

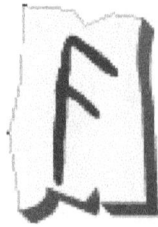

Ansuz

If Ansuz is your Heart Rune, you have an uncanny knack of hearing and integrating your own inner wisdom and the wisdom of the Universe. You have help in the form of spirit guides and helpers, which means that often what refuses to work for others will somehow work for you.

A main challenge to you if Ansuz is your Heart Rune is concerned with listening and hearing. It may be so easy for you to hear messages from the Universe that you may develop a habit of hearing "for" others and interpreting for them what they need to interpret for themselves. If you find that you are constantly being offered advice, Ansuz may be urging you to define your own sense of self and find ways to speak your truth.

Remember that just because hearing is a talent of yours, that doesn't mean that if others hear differently that they are wrong. If you are a teacher or a parent, you may be an excellent teacher but you could have a tendency to help your children or students too much. Have faith in them and in the Universe's ability to lead them.

Ansuz is connected to the Throat and Third Eye Chakras, which helps you to know when to speak and when to be silent, as well as what words to use. The optimal path is to listen first to your inner wisdom and the wisdom that comes from the Universe through your Third Eye, and share from that perspective.

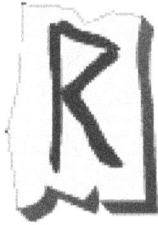

Raido

Raido is the Rune of Journey, Communication and Expertise. Having Raido as a Heart Rune indicates a life full of adventure, learning, sharing, travel, refining of skills and communion on the human and Divine levels.

Raido is also concerned with developing enough expertise to create a balanced life. This may manifest itself in many opportunities to learn. You may feel like you are a perpetual student but just at the right moment you will have the necessary piece to complete a project you're involved with or to allow you to find the flexibility and resources you need to complete it.

People with Raido as a Heart Rune tend to have a life focus of balance and more finely attuning their inner and outer selves. This means that you may see others get away with much more than you are able to get away with.

You will also find it difficult to align yourself with a single point of view. Thankfully, Raido provides enough strength for you to stand on your own, as well as the perspective not to be concerned if you don't belong to a specific group. The ability to see both sides of a situation gives you a broader perspective and more flexibility even though it also can make it more difficult for you to be a part of a specific group.

This helps you in two ways: 1) By showing you how transient and therefore, precious, the encounters in life are, which enables you to hold dear those who are in your life while giving you the flexibility to let them go when your time together is done, and 2) To be able to create agreement and when two groups of people are so polarized that it's difficult for them to see any point of view except their own.

People may complain that you are never "on their side" but they will be glad that someone has a broader perspective when negotiations reach a deadlock—which is something Raido people never reach because their ability to see many aspects at once helps to keep them moving. Raido Heart Rune people also help to raise the vibration of the world by reminding others to feel a deep connection to nature and the Universe.

The connection to the Root and Sacral Chakras gives Raido people a sense of deep groundedness that gives them the flexibility to keep learning and keep moving even when life presents stress or obstacles.

The main focus of Raido energy is that of self-healing. That means this present life is one of healing, upward movement, learning to ride the thermals like an eagle. Raido people tend to have recurring health issues. Others may be able to get away with eating junk food once in awhile, but the systems of Radio energy people tend to let them know very quickly if they are out of balance. Stomach issues, ulcers, digestive complaints, allergies and nervous conditions are all warnings that you need to bring yourself back into balance.

Raido also reminds you that joy is always present in life, regardless of the circumstances. Remove the slanted line beneath Raido's triangular-shaped 'head' and you are left with Wunjo, Rune of Joy. Wunjo reminds you that though you may feel as if you have had a long journey, the end is always in sight and the end of the journey is joy.

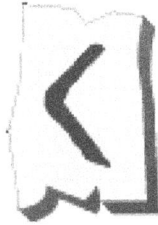

Kano

Kano is the Rune of the open door, the kind of opening that brings transformative knowledge. People who have Kano as a Heart Rune tend to be open-minded, generous and caring. Kano offers the opportunity for light to enter places that have been kept in the dark. This translates into opportunities for you to bring joy into others' lives by knowing just what words to say or what gift to bring to a party.

Kano people also tend to have the needed ingredient, insight or skill to fill a need, which not only helps others but brings the opportunity for prosperity and happiness to them as well.

Though there isn't a real downside to having Kano energy as a main energetic thread in your life, the keen vision that comes with Kano's energy can cause you to notice even the smallest discrepancies. This can be helpful if you are gentle and respectful in pointing out omissions and if you have a good sense of balance about what is worth standing up for and what is best let go.

Kano people are also known for their sharp wit, which can make you fun to be around, providing you allow yourself to be sensitive enough not to step on too many toes. A main challenge for Kano people is sensitivity. You are much more comfortable standing in the bright light of laser-sharp awareness than your friends may be, so be aware of how your observations may affect others.

Kano people can tend to be critical if their energy is low

or if they are depressed. Remember that though you have been gifted with clear sight, you still have to live out this life in cooperation with others.

Kano energy is connected to the Root and Sacral Chakras. Your clarity of thought and vision can help you to create a very secure, grounded place in this life. Your vision can also help you to create new products, companies, ideas and bring them into being.

If your Root and/or Sacral Chakra is weak, you may feel as if your vision is working against you. You may notice more things "wrong" about the world than "right" and get stuck when you are challenged to make positive changes.

Gebo

Gebo is the Rune of Partnerships of all kinds and of gifts, especially energetic exchanges. People with Gebo as a heart Rune know how to join with others and/or with causes without losing their sense of individuality or self, while being of benefit in the relationship or cause. This is why Gebo looks like an "X." The two lines are equal yet they touch at the heart.

Gebo people are usually easy going. They prefer to watch and wait when stressors appear because they know that ultimately, everything will work out. This is because Gebo people have a deep understanding of one of the core truths about how the Universe works: That in the end, all things must balance out.

This perspective gives Gebo people the gift of freedom by helping them have an open mind and also have an understanding of what it means to hold onto the physical aspects of life lightly while deeply valuing the spiritual and human connections.

Gebo's open energy is shown by the open ends on the top and bottom of the "X" shape that forms this Rune. Gebo people know that life itself is a partnership, and that all gifts come from finding the balance and equality in life. Though they may at times be criticized for not taking sides, they know that they will receive more rewards from life by remaining in balance rather than fighting or resisting life.

Gebo people are gifted in many areas—artistically, intuitively and financially. As long as they stay balanced,

193

they find anything they need. In an ultimate sense, Gebo people see life's journey as a matter of finesse and balance, emerging from a union with the Divine, and ending in the present life again as union with the Divine.

Gebo's energy is connected to the Throat and Third Eye Chakras. This indicates the clarity of vision can combine with the ability to speak into circumstances of potential stress to create peace and balance. This also indicates that if you are having challenges, that you can resolve them by relying more on your intuition and your connection to the Universe, and letting that wisdom help you to speak your truth.

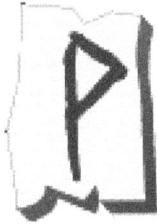

Wunjo

If Wunjo is a Heart Rune for you, this indicates that you know and accept yourself at a deep level. You are at peace with yourself and that peace manifests as a resonance of joy that draws others to you.

This strong sense of inner joy causes everything you do to bear fruit of one sort or another. Even when life is challenging or stressful, Wunjo's energy is so joyful that you are able to find ways to make the best of things, a little like making lemonade or using bitter spring herbs for cleansing.

Wunjo's energy gives you a strong passion for life, where shifts and changes feel exhilarating instead of exhausting. If Wunjo is your Heart Rune, this indicates that you have lived many lives and have learned enough soul lessons to live this present life with a deep sense of satisfaction.

Some of the shifts of Wunjo may be energetic shifts in awareness, understanding and growth that you have waited for many lifetimes to achieve. This life is a time to receive Wunjo's many blessings and to feel more at home in yourself than you have ever felt before.

You use your highly-developed sense of self-awareness to understand how to find the people, ideas and resources in your present life to fulfill your goals. Your sense of self is so unshakable that when you face difficult challenges you know that everything will work out. You will be carried across that gap by the updrafts created by Wunjo's joy.

Whenever your energy is blocked, by illness, life circumstances or other challenges, you find ways to open up the flow for whatever you need. Even in times of difficulty, you aren't worried because you know that your soul is illuminated from within.

People with Wunjo as a Heart Rune are clear thinking, excellent planners, and able to fulfill their goals and dreams. You have excellent vision and amazing ability to manifest.

Wunjo energy is tied to the Throat Chakra, allowing you to give voice to your deepest hopes and use the energy of being itself to carry you through the ups and downs of physical life.

Hagalaz

People with Hagalz as a Heart Rune tend to be strong-willed. They don't allow anything to stop them from implementing the changes they need to make. Freedom is very important to them, so they chafe under any constricting beliefs or expectations that cause them to feel as if they need to do what is expected rather than how they truly feel they need to act. Even if the changes cause them inconvenience or discomfort, or cause others to turn away from them, Hagalaz people will make the change because they can see the connection to the ultimate growth.

Hagalz people think best with an archetypal mind—one that sees the world in themes, energy vibrations and mythic analogies rather than taking things personally. Hagalz is also called the Great Awakener because its energy will not tolerate falsehood, insincerity or untruths. Hagalz people abide by the Universal rules and use them as their structure. Hagalz people try to cooperate with human rules also, as much as they agree with Universal ones, more for a sense of structure than from a sense that human rules are ultimately the best.

Hagalaz people also tend to rip apart the existing structure of their lives when necessary, which, when done unconsciously, can make it seem as if uncontrollable forces are shredding their world. But Hagalz people are sturdy and stable, and eventually find their footing again. Realizing that they are the source of their disruptions helps Hagalz people not only accept life's upheavals, but also teaches them to use the changing energies the way a surfer uses the power of the waves.

Hagalaz people are strong in will, intent and spirit if not always in body. No matter the level of disruption, they know they always have a choice in how to see the disruption and what to do about it. They know they are never powerless and that ultimately, all disruptions help their spirit to grow.

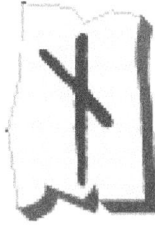

Nauthiz

Nauthiz is the Rune of pain and constraint that lead to a greater sense of self-empowerment. People drawn to Nauthiz may often find themselves learning to deal with illness, disability, pain and other constricting barriers. Nauthiz energy is interesting. It can represent snags and obstacles we create as well as those that we encounter in the greater world.

Since we know that we create our own experiences, though, Nauthiz urges you to go to the root of whatever is frustrating you or slowing you down. See what you can do, what skills you can learn, what attitudes you can shift, to make your life less painful.

If Nauthiz is your Heart Rune, the Universe is trying to show you that the frustrations, constraints and difficulties that may make you feel doomed are intended to provide the energy to help you see how your own energy draws similar energy to you. Once you are aware of the shadowy aspects of your inner self, it will be much easier for you to see how and why you are drawing hardship to you.

People with Nauthiz as a Heart Rune may indicate the need for deliberate intent and caution instead of moving too quickly when making plans. A benefit of Nauthiz energy is that you have ample opportunities to learn perseverance and good humor as the Rune of Constraint teaches you balance. You know how to mend, restore and bring into harmony both yourself and everything around you. Nauthiz teaches that if one thing doesn't work, try something else. Your versatility assures that you never need to feel like you are without choices, no matter the circumstances.

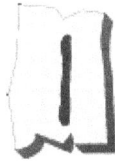

Isa

Isa is concerned with stillness. That can indicate a life filled with stops and starts, but at its heart, Isa energy is the energy of contemplation, specifically the energy of the Contemplative Mind.

If Isa is your Heart Rune, any little thing may seem to slow you down or stop you. You may get frustrated as everyone else seems to skate through life without a care, while you flounder and are forced to stop again and again.

The key is to look to the energy of Isa. What you are being asked to do is not to stop, but to take time to contemplate the deep nature of yourself and of your life. If you do this, instead of feeling stuck, you will learn deep wisdom that will be a tool you can use to guide you through life.

Of course, if Isa's true challenge to dive deep is not recognized, you may find yourself literally stuck—isolated in a small town, separated from those you love, unable to find a way to get the education you need—you name it. But once you give Isa energy the time and respect it asks for, the opposite will be true.

Your wisdom will increase. You will have the opportunity to be with people or be alone, as you have need. People will see you as a profound person, a calm and contemplative, peaceful person. Great are the benefits of having Isa as a Heart Rune, to be sure.

Jera

If Jera has turned up as your Heart Rune, you may be deeply tied to the cycles of life and death, growth, harvest and rebirth. You may feel a deep connection to the Earth and to the seasons.

What Jera is asking of you is to pay special attention in this lifetime to the cycles of life. In fact, all aspects of timing will be important to you in this lifetime. This is the knife's edge of Jera energy: If you pay attention to the cycles of life and of nature, your life will contain many cycles of growth, satisfaction and abundance.

If you don't pay enough attention to life cycles and get ahead of yourself, or behind the current cycle, you'll miss opportunities that can leave you feeling as if you are "off."

If Jera is your Heart Rune, you are probably confident and good in a crisis, since the underlying energy of your life philosophy, the core of your inner laws, so to speak, is that you know that everything works out in the end and that all cycles will play out no matter how bleak or chaotic things may look along the way.

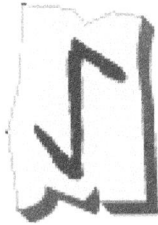

Eihwaz

If Eihwaz is your Heart Rune, you may be an excellent chess player because you tend to see games and life events three or four, or more, moves ahead of others. This allows you to develop an effective defense when you need it, because you have a knack of taking note of details, nuances and patterns in a way that helps you to anticipate what will happen later on.

In other words, you tend to see trouble before it arrives, which gives you plenty of time to get out of the way. Eihwaz' energy offers you the ability to be flexible enough have the power to defeat external or internal foes. Part of the reason for this is the ability Eihwaz energy gives you to take an objective stance. A friend or colleague may be melting down but what you are listening for are opportunities for stability and harmony.

This perspective works in your favor whether you are facing financial, relationship or health-related stress. Others may marvel, for example, at a study that finds eating fiber to strengthen the digestive system but to you this is common sense.

So much of life is common sense for you, in fact, that if you are careful, you can create a position for yourself where people come to you for advice. Eihwaz people are excellent advisors, judges, counselors, referees, CEOs and pastors. Your skill in being able to see far enough ahead to see the consequences not only spares you from a lot of life's troubles, but it helps you to guide others through life as well.

Perth

If Perth is your Heart Rune, you are good at keeping secrets. So good, in fact, that people may be drawn to you to confide in you with issues that they don't feel confident entrusting others with. Part of the reason for this is your easygoing nature. No matter what comes at you, you manage to stay afloat.

Perth also has a tendency to introduce you to new patterns and new cycles. This keeps you on the leading edge, so to speak, depending on how well you're able to rise to the challenge of Perth's constant cycle of the newest, most innovative and most motivating.

A challenge that Perth throws your way is the feeling that you are constantly in the state of barely getting used to the latest pattern before a new pattern is offered. Perth doesn't allow you to get bored or become too comfortable, but if you rise to the challenges offered by Perth's energy, your life will be a series of steps that lead you to new heights in your path of healing and growth.

Because Perth is also a mystery Rune or a Rune of Secrets, you may be able to see far enough ahead of the curve that others may not understand why, for example, you choose to leave a successful company where you have a stable job for a speculative opportunity. But the powerful forces of change that Perth sends into your life soon prove that you made the right decision.

The changes Perth offers can come as a sudden insight, perhaps a clever way of streamlining a system or a unique way of accomplishing an everyday task. Perth's association with the Phoenix, a sacred, mythical firebird spirit with colorful plumage and a golden tail, can also mean that just when others are sure you will fail, you rise up into a new job, relationship or area of life that allows you to be happy and fulfilled.

Though Perth can be an uncomfortable Runic energy to have as a Heart Rune, it ensures a life filled with challenge, excitement, achievement and growth.

Algiz

If Algiz is your Heart Rune, you are either very good at creating healthy boundaries or are provided with opportunities to create healthy boundaries over and over until you master this important skill.

It may seem a bit unfair, for example, that others get away with doing a little less thorough of a job than you do, but if you miss even one detail, you are called on it. Another way Algiz challenges you to develop boundaries is by allowing people to be drawn to you who will ask to borrow things, or who you can't even share your house or yard with, without them asking to have this or that.

Instead of getting annoyed at the people, be aware that Algiz is challenging you to create clear boundaries. The energy of Algiz is the most powerfully defensive energy of all the Runes. Though you will be at times challenged by people thinking your house is the neighborhood grocery store, once you clarify your boundaries, you will be able to get along without resentment or arguments.

It's important to note that boundary breaches are more of an annoyance and an attention-getter, like the rustle of grass or a rattlesnake's rattle. The issue it to create enough clear space around you so that you have room to breathe. Setting boundaries doesn't mean pushing everyone away.

The most important thing to consider when Algiz energy enters your life is to keep your cool. If you need to create more personal space or set boundaries, doing so from a place of calm, clear emotional energy will help.

Sowelu

If Sowelu is your Heart Rune, the main focus of your life will be on completion and wholeness. This can mean anything from wanting to see a tough job through to attending dozens of self-help classes to ensure that you are the best person you can be. In other words, getting to know yourself and creating a unique face to present to the world will be extremely important to you.

Since Sowelu offers a strong energy of life force and self-realization, your deepest hope may be to express to a profound recognition of your true self that is recognized by your friends, family, coworkers and perhaps by the world as a whole.

And if world recognitions is your goal, Sowelu's clear, focused energy helps you by giving you an awareness of the absolute certainty that you came to this life, in this place and time, for a specific reason. There is no doubt in your mind of the importance of your existence.

Since Sowelu is a sun Rune, its focus is on reaching the pinnacle of your soul's overall quest. This is a conscious recognition that allows you to face challenges with an eagerness that can cause others to shake their heads. This absolute certainty comes from your profound recognition of yourself that removes any doubts as to your abilities and gives you the strength to say no to stressful situations and people, instead of hiding your true feelings in an effort to be polite.

Teiwaz

If Teiwaz is your Heart Rune, you have the spirit of a warrior. Specifically, you are in close contact with your own inner energies to the point where you can control your emotions and focus your thoughts.

Teiwaz' energy ensures no matter what happens, you will find a way to handle it. Even if you are provoked, you choose your battles wisely, because you know that battle is always with the self, not with the outside forces that seem to be enticing you to fight.

As a warrior Rune, Teiwaz provides you with weapons and tools that you can use to help you get through life. One of the weapons Teiwaz offers is the power of the observer. You have the ability to watch the events around you without taking the specific aspects personally. Even if it feels as if someone is punching your buttons, you never lose sight of your own inner energy.

This perspective gives you a depth and sense of compassion, which helps you to offer unexpected insights that can defuse a potentially explosive situation.

Another tool Teiwaz offers is that of patience. Once you have learned to be patient with yourself, it is much easier to be patient with others.

A third tool Teiwaz offers is that of balance. You aren't likely to rush out to a sale, for example, unless you really need the items being offered. The tool of balance can also help you to know when it's time to let go, and when you have enough. This knowledge can keep you out of arguments, debates and competitive races while letting you know the perfect moment to jump in.

Berkana

If Berkana, the Rune of Growth and Rising Vibrations, is your Heart Rune, a main theme of your life will be growth. This can be the kind of growth that comes from lessons learned, from natural talent or a challenging growth that needs to be monitored to keep it balanced.

The bottom line is that Berkana's energy helps to raise your inner and outer vibrations. Berkana's season is spring, when plants and animals awaken after their winter's sleep and fertility once again fills the world.

If Berkana is your Heart Rune, it is important for you to clearly state what you do and do not want, because whatever projects you begin or goals you set now will grow at a rapid pace.

This rapid growth can be a good thing, providing the things that are growing are things you really want. For example, if you are starting a business, be sure you really love what you are doing. If you are planting a garden, plant flowers, fruits, vegetables and other plants that you like. Whatever you do, plan carefully.

Berkana energy also challenges you to remain calm and centered. Growth of all kinds will be attracted to you, so be aware of what you are attracting. Your ideas will sizzle, bringing all kinds of people your way. Avoid drama or conflicts, especially those having to do with opinion, because whatever energies you attract will grow. That includes productive energies like diligence and honesty as well as energies of anger, greed or competition. Don't let things get blown out of proportion. Remember to prune away anything that you don't want growing in your life.

Ehwaz

Ehwaz is the Rune of Movement and the Unbreakable Bond. If Ehwaz is your Heart Rune, your life will be filled with steady, forward movement and growth. This may make you feel at times as if you aren't moving fast enough or as if you're treading water, but though the steps you're taking may seem small, the steadiness of the growth is one of Ehwaz's blessings.

Since Ehwaz energy is also connected to transportation, you may have a knack of choosing just the right car, planning the most interesting stops on trips, or booking the optimal flights.

Physical or energetic shifts may be easier for you to make than for others as well. Shifts like a change of heart, a paradigm shift or ability to grasp new technology can help you to move forward or keep up with the momentum of life.

Ehwaz's physical shifts can include new homes, giving you the perspective and savvy to navigate the real estate arena. If you need a home, you may have a knack of choosing the right time to buy, or to sell a home you own. You may even choose to be a real estate agent and help others to find an ideal home.

Ehwaz's steady progress gives you a sense of stability that comes from having enough life experience to know how to transport yourself not just when you need to travel or move to a new home, but through life itself. This stability helps you to build a large enough financial base so that you have enough to share with others.

Ehwaz also offers the patience and clarity to clear up a misunderstanding. This is partly due to the fact that Ehwaz's consistent incremental growth helps you build patience. Ehwaz helps you to create not only a stable life, but stable, long-lasting friendships as well.

Mannez

Mannez is Rune of the Self and the Source. If Mannez is your Heart Rune, you will find yourself at the center of things. You may be the center of attention, the creator of an idea, video or company that goes viral, or, if you allow yourself to become unbalanced, the center of a controversy or scandal.

The main challenge Mannez offers is to teach you the importance of having a healthy, balanced relationship with yourself. Balance requires expertise and patience so at times when you may be tempted to rush through a project, remember to keep a balanced perspective. Another main challenge may be to develop a clear sense of who you are.

Mannez reminds you that you don't need to feel rushed or stressed. You just need to be you. This is the core of Mannez, that you are enough just as you are. The key to being who you are is acceptance. The key of acceptance is to live in the present. If living in the moment seems scary or even boring to you, remember that hidden within your daily tasks is the core of joy for your life.

Whenever you feel alone, as if you have no one to lean on, Mannez reminds you that you have inner support. It may seem logical that others help to balance you but ultimately it is the self that balances and supports the self. In other words, when your inner world is at peace with the outer world, your life will be in balance.

Laguz

If Laguz is your Heart Rune, your life will be as fluid and changeable as water. This may make you feel a bit uncertain until you get your sea legs, so to speak. Laguz energy is that of the rising and falling of the tides of life, reminding you that no matter what is going on at the surface of your life, you have hidden depths and powers that keep your energy flowing and help things work out in the end.

Laguz' energy challenges you to focus on the energetic flow of life: emotions, careers, relationships, plans, life cycles. A key to learning to ride Laguz's currents is to live without judging or scrutinizing yourself or others.

As a lunar Rune, Laguz connects you deeply to your intuitive self, reminding you that if you listen to your inner wisdom, your life will flow in harmony with the Universe itself.

Laguz energy can also help you organize or reorganize your life. The organization can be anything from physically cleaning up your home and work space, or energetic practices such as meditation. This reorganization is to help you prepare for self-transformation.

Laguz is sometimes called the happily ever after Rune because it brings you to the place of what alchemists call the conjunctio[29] or sacred marriage, where you have worked

---

[29] Blum, Ralph, The Book of Runes, p. 127.

through your life challenges and will now live happily ever after.

Inguz: Rune of the Beacon of Light

If Inguz is your Heart Rune, you often experience powerful dreams. In fact, you may be so well-connected intuitively that others come to you for energetic support. People with Inguz as a Heart Rune are sensitive to the needs of others and intuitively know how to offer appropriate help. You're probably intuitive enough to be a psychic, counselor, judge or medium. The Inguz person is warm, cheerful, sharing, kind and deeply spiritual.

Inguz energy is also harmonizing, giving you a sense of inner support that helps you connect with others in the outer world in a balanced way. Inguz energy holds a core of joy that carries you though many difficult situations because it gives you a foundational belief that no matter what, everything will work out in the end.

This fundamental belief makes it easier for you to start over whenever you reach a new life cycle or at times when you need to grow. Inguz gives you the perspective of self-reliance by reminding you that you must take care of your own life so that you have something of value to offer to others.

One of Inguz's strongest energetic threads is that of completion. Inguz helps you to complete each life cycle, project or promise, until at last your life's journey itself is complete. Once you have finished your time in the mortal realms, you are ready to once again head to the Universe, so your soul enjoys a spate of peace and respite before once again plunging into human life.

Inguz is also the Rune of emergence, giving you periods of quiet time to learn and grow, and then urging you to share what you know with the world.

Dagaz

If Dagaz is your Heart Rune, it may seem as if you are riding the rapids of life, as it were. Dagaz brings into your life the energy of breakthrough, which can lead to transformation including major shifts in belief and thinking, if you allow it.

As a Sun Rune, Dagaz's strong yang energy urges you to discover yourself and not to be afraid of being yourself. The more willing you are to stand out from the crowd will determine the kinds of breakthroughs you experience. You may be a visionary who introduces a new way of thinking to the world or you may prefer to work more quietly, transforming your life from the inside.

With Dagaz as a Heart Rune, you can be single-minded, going for broke in the area of change. Yet that doesn't mean you approach change blindly. You know the work ahead of you and take the time and effort necessary to plan carefully, and then make your moves with dazzling speed and accuracy.

Dagaz helps you to know that no matter what physical things are disturbed by your growth, you are always reaching sunwards so you don't worry too much about the fallout. You are expert at knowing just the right time to buy, sell, move or seize an opportunity.

This is because your trust is based on Universal laws rather than on the stock market or oil prices. You know when you need to move forward, even if it seems that everyone else is holding back. In short, you are a master of your own world.

Othila

Othila is the Rune of Energetic Fences. If Othila is your Heart Rune, your life will be filled with boundary issues. Land disputes, fences, misunderstandings, the possibility of enmeshment or even abuse; all are challenges of Othila's energy.

These challenges are not a bad thing. They are simply a message from the Universe that in this lifetime, a main focus will be on the creating and maintaining of boundaries. Boundaries are easier to maintain if you see them as an energetic fence. Even though boundaries are invisible, they can be clearly felt. As soon as you learn how to set effective boundaries, you'll realize that the energy of Othila has helped you to create a strong space that no one can take from you.

The reason that boundaries are so important on a Universal level is because they are the foundations of beliefs and ideas that can last many lifetimes. Your boundaries speak to your deepest beliefs about how much value you place in your life. Once you know what you value, creating an appropriate amount of space around you will be much easier.

Other challenges Othila offers you are of clarity and objectivity. Don't be afraid to state what you need clearly, and don't make exceptions. An everyday example of a boundary is a stop sign. The message behind the stop sign is very clear, and no matter how familiar you are with the area where the stop sign is located, you still need to stop. The same goes for your boundaries.

If Othila is your Heart Rune, you may have entered this life as a member of a dysfunctional family, to give you the opportunity to break a generational pattern. For example, if you have been told all your life that you don't have the right to have an opinion, setting boundaries might be challenging for you. But until you begin to set boundaries, people don't have a sense of who you are. Though there is risk of rejection if you do dare to claim your space, doing so will also give you a better sense of who you are.

Odin

Odin is the Rune of Unlimited Potential. If Odin is your Heart Rune, you are a Star Child. Your life may feel open-ended or you may even feel out of place. You may often find yourself in situations where it feels as if you can go in any direction. Though you may seek guidance, you are left again and again on your own. The more willing you are to stand or fall on your convictions rather than go with the crowd, the more you will be able to benefit from Odin's open-ended energy.

Odin gives you a stronger connection with the Divine than to physical possessions like houses, furnishings or jobs. It may be difficult for you to trust people because the rules that people create tend to be much more restrictive and subjective than Universal Laws. Yet Odin asks you to do the illogical—leap empty-handed into the Void, which can land you either on the side of the Universe or the side of humanity.

Odin was the first Rune pulled for me. At that time in my life, this Rune spoke deeply to my heart, reminding me that I wasn't alone, that even when there were more loose ends than I could count, that a Universal plan really was guiding my life. The Odin Rune reminded me that not only did I know the Source, but that the core of my being was part of the Source.

If Odin is your Heart Rune, your deep connection to Universal Laws may cause you to appear uncooperative to others, because you do not simply give in to other people or go along with the crowd without being sure that is exactly what you want to do. If you are wise, you will learn to cooperate with rather than obey humankind. If you are patient and objective, you will see that most people will give in to the Universe if given the chance.

Being familiar with a sense of ambiguity doesn't mean you are unfamiliar with fear. In fact, you have faced so many challenges that you have learned to uncover and master your deepest hidden fears. You know fear the way a polar bear knows cold. It is familiar but not dangerous and is an indicator rather than an obstacle.

This familiarity with fear allows you to have the flexibility to focus on the greatest good and the purest intent instead of just doing the minimum. Your deepest belief is in the unlimited potential of the human heart and spirit, without losing sight of your connection to the Divine and to your higher self. You know that nothing is lost forever. Even painful losses are a reminder of the connection to the Divine and to other realms of living.

Chapter 16:
Finding Runes in Everyday Life

Though we may not realize it, the energy of the Runes is always around us. One way to recognize and call the energy of Runes into play in your daily life is to look for Runic symbols in the objects around you.

For example, every morning when I shower, I see the Runes Mannez and Ehwaz in the textured walls above my bathtub. Mannez is a constant reminder to me to maintain an inner and outer balance, both claiming my humanity and embracing my connection to other humans.

Wunjo is embedded in the Rune Mannez, reminding me to look for reasons to feel and express joy and gratitude in each day.

Ehwaz reminds me that even on days when it seems that I make little progress, that the steady, forward motion will ultimately help me reach my goals. This Rune also reminds me that Universal Law works the same for me as it does for everyone else. This is especially helpful during times when misunderstandings and miscommunication snarl my energy.

My husband is reminded daily of the benefits and messages contained in the Rune Uruz. He has done a lot of work with his hands over his lifetime, and several small scars on his left hand form the shape of the Rune Uruz. This reminds him that his inner and outer strength has been honed over the years, and also serves as a reminder for him to consider his own needs so that he doesn't exceed the strength he has developed and create more scars.

As you go about your day, look for Rune Symbols etched into the bark of trees, in traffic signs such as arrows and X's, in puddles or drops of water on the hood of your car. Just as considering the messages contained in repetitive thoughts, number sequences and other patterns can be helpful, taking a few moments to consider the wisdom contained in any Rune Symbols you encounter can help you to live each day with wisdom and grace.

Another way to use the messages of the Runes in your everyday life is to pay attention to your energy. If you feel closed off, for example, you can invite the opening energy of Kano or Gebo into your life. Draw or picture Kano and/or Gebo's symbol, then imagine the energy of the Runes entering the part of your life that feels stuck.

The stuckness can manifest as a sore back, frustration or as small or large setbacks in your life. As you invite the energy of Kano of Gebo into those areas, feel its gentle currents wearing away the blockages just as a stream will wear away the rough edges of the stones that lie on its beds. Soon your life will begin to flow more smoothly as well.

If you feel stuck financially, invite the energy of Fehu into your life. Remember that Fehu asks you to consider what the real rewards and profits are in your life—in short, what is most important to you?

Once you are able to see what you really value, your path should be clearer to find your way to success and plenty.

If you are beginning a new venture, invite the energy of Gebo, Gera or Inguz into your life, for a successful completion of the project as well as the ability to sustain stead forward progress.

If you feel challenged to break new ground or learn a new skill, invite the watery flow of Laguz and/or the breakthrough energy of Dagaz. If you need to create boundaries or make a break from distressing energies, invite the wisdom of Othila, Uruz and/or Hagalaz into your life.

Incorporating Runic wisdom into your daily life will increase your knowledge of the Runes themselves as well as give you the insight you need to live a full, abundant life.

Bibliography

Blum, Ralph H, *The Book of Runes*, St. Martin's Press, New York, 1993.

A Muse-ing Grace Gallery: The Magical Art of Thalia Took, http://www.thaliatook.com/AMGG/skuld.html

Bible, Women's Devotional, New International Version, Zondervan Publishing House, Grand Rapids, MI, 1994.

God Checker: Norse Mythology, the Mighty Gods of the Vikings, http://www.godchecker.com/pantheon/norse-mythology.php?deity=BALDUR

Heimdallr, http://en.wikipedia.org/wiki/Heimdall

LikeMindz: Rune Meanings by Yankee, LikeMindz.com.

Kaptchuk, Ted J. *The Web That Has No Weaver: Understanding Chinese Medicine*, Contemporary Books, New York, NY, 2000.

Mother Holda, http://en.wikipedia.org/wiki/Frau_Holda

Nine Mothers of Heimdallr, http://en.wikipedia.org/wiki/Nine_Mothers_of_Heimdallr

Njoror, http://en.wikipedia.org/wiki/Njörðr

Odin, http://en.wikipedia.org/wiki/Odin

Ogam, http://www.encyclopedia.com/doc/1O245-ogam.html

PaganLore.com, http://paganlore.com/rune-ngpage.aspx

Pennick, Nigel, *The Complete Illustrated Guide to Runes: How to Interpret the Ancient Wisdom of the Runes*. Element Books Ltd, Boston, MA, 1999

Rand, William Lee, *Reiki: The Healing Touch. First and Second Degree Manual.* Vision Publications, Southfield, MI, 2008.

Runes: Alphabet of Mystery, http://www.sunnyway.com/runes/mythology.html

Rune web vitki: Rune Lore, http://runewebvitki.com/Rune%20Lore.htm

The Wild Hunt, http://en.wikipedia.org/wiki/Wild_Hunt.

Tyson, Donald, *Rune Magic.* Llewellyn Publications, St. Paul, MN, 1988.

Willis, Tony, *Discover Runes: Understanding and Using the Power of Runes.* Sterling Publishing Company, New York, NY, 1993.

About the Author

Kriss Erickson is a versatile freelance writer with over 1,000 published pieces to date. Some of her previous works are: *Sky Eyes: Dissociative Identity Disorder from the Bottom Up* and the *Land Behind the Veil* fantasy series, both available through AKW Books as e-books.

Kriss is also a certified counselor, owner of Rising Spirals Reiki and a Usui/Tibetan, Atlantean, Crystal, Karuna (tm), Ra-Sheeba, Shamanic and Lightarian (tm) Reiki Master Teacher, AngelLinks and Cosmic Ray Facilitator and Level III Acutonics (tm) Practitioner. She writes and works from her home in Everett, WA.